THE TRIUMPH OF LOVE

THE TRIUMPH OF LOVE

SAMUEL SANNI

Published by SLF Press
Calgary AB, Canada
ISBN: 978-1-0691195-0-6 - Book
ISBN: 978-1-0691195-1-3 - Ebook

For more information, contact:
info@supernaturallifeforum.com
www.supernaturallifeforum.com

CONTENTS

DEDICATION

To the Triune God—Father, Son, and Holy Spirit—whose boundless love, infinite grace, and unwavering faithfulness inspire this work. May this book be a testament to Your glorious truth and an echo of the hope You offer to all creation through the cross of Christ.

To my beloved wife, Olatundun, whose unwavering support, love, and encouragement have been my greatest strength. Your faith and partnership in this journey have illuminated the path and made this endeavor possible.

And to my cherished children, Jesuleke and Hadassah, whose joy, curiosity, and love remind me daily of the profound beauty and promise of God's kingdom. May this book be a gift to you, a reflection of the hope we hold in Christ, and a legacy of the truth and love that define our lives.

With deepest gratitude and affection,
Samuel Sanni

Preface

In a world often overshadowed by fear and uncertainty regarding the afterlife, the message of hope and redemption found in the Gospel of Jesus Christ offers a beacon of light. This book emerges from a profound journey into the heart of biblical and societal reflection, aimed at reconciling the depth of God's love with the concept of what happened after life and the broader implications of salvation.

Many times, the Church, which was supposed to be an oasis in the desert and an avenue of hope, has become a place where the little hope that society has is eroded. It has become a place where people lose the trust they have in God. Unbelief and doubt have multiplied because of the teachings and preaching of the Church. This is despite the fact that Christian teachings from the early Church and the early Fathers are quite different from the modern Church's teachings. The Gospel has been so perverted by the modern Church that the real Gospel is unidentifiable to the majority of churchgoers.

The inspiration for this work stems from a deep-seated conviction that the love of God, as revealed through the incarnation, life, death, resurrection and ascension of Jesus Christ, is not only transformative for our present world but also extends its reach into the realms of the afterlife. This conviction compels us to explore the possibility that divine mercy may indeed encompass more than we have traditionally understood, challenging the conventional notions of eternal punishment and embracing a more hopeful and inclusive vision of salvation.

As we delve into the intricacies of eschatology; the doctrine of the last things and the nature of hell, we encounter the tension between traditional doctrines of eternal retribution and a more expansive view of God's restorative justice. This book seeks to navigate these complexities, presenting a balanced perspective that honors the integrity of Scripture and the revelation of the nature of God through Christ while inviting readers to consider a broader, more hopeful understanding of God's ultimate plan for humanity.

Each chapter builds upon a foundation of biblical exegesis and theological reflection, drawing from the rich heritage of early church fathers and contemporary scholars. The exploration begins with the profound love of God revealed in Christ, moves through the challenging concept of hell, and culminates in a vision of redemption and victory that is both rooted in Scripture and inspired by the enduring hope of the Gospel.

In engaging with these themes, this book does not seek to diminish the gravity of divine justice or the reality of judgment but to offer a perspective that harmonizes these elements with the overarching message of divine love and redemption. By presenting a hopeful and very inclusive vision of salvation, I aim to provide a more comprehensive understanding of God's work in the world and in the lives of individuals.

Moreover, this work is intended to encourage readers to reflect on their own beliefs about salvation, judgment, and the nature of God's love. It challenges us to consider how our understanding of these concepts affects our view of God and our relationship with others. It is my hope that the insights presented here will lead to a deeper appreciation of the profound truths of the Gospel, inspire a renewed commitment to living out the message of love and hope, and foster a greater sense of unity and compassion within the Christian community.

As you journey through these pages, may you find assurance in the expansive mercy and grace of God, hope in the promise of salvation, and a renewed sense of purpose in living out the Gospel message. It is my hope that the insights presented here will challenge, inspire, and uplift, leading you to a deeper understanding of the profound truths of God's love and the ultimate victory achieved through Christ's cross.

Welcome to a journey of faith, hope, and redemption. As we embark on this exploration together, may we be guided by the light of Christ's love, empowered by the hope of His victory, and transformed by the promise of salvation that extends beyond the bounds of this present age.

Samuel Sanni
Calgary, 2024

Introduction

Divine Love and the Hope of Life

In the grand narrative of human existence, the profound questions of life, death, and destiny have always stirred the deepest corners of our hearts. Amid the uncertainties and struggles that mark our journey, there is a resounding beacon of hope that illuminates the path forward: the love of God in Christ and the promise of eternal salvation. This book embarks on a journey through the transformative power of the Gospel, exploring the depths of divine love, the ultimate victory of God in Christ Jesus, and the possibility of hope that transcends even the boundaries of death.

The Triumph of Divine Love

At the heart of the Christian message is the astonishing truth that God's love, as revealed in Jesus Christ, is both infinite and transformative. This love, profound and unchanging, reaches beyond the limits of human understanding and embraces every aspect of our existence. It is a love that does not merely tolerate but actively redeems and restores. The cross of Christ stands as the ultimate symbol of this love—an emblem of sacrificial grace that conquers sin, overcomes death, and offers the promise of eternal life. *For God so loved the world that He gave His only begotten Son, that whoever believes in Him should not perish but have everlasting life* John 3:16 KJV. This verse captures the essence of divine love—an unconditional, all-encompassing love that extends to every corner of creation. The cross of Christ, in what looks like a defeat, becomes the very instrument of God's ultimate victory. In the suffering and sacrifice of Christ, we find the greatest expression of divine love—a love that absorbs the weight of human sin and transforms it into a gateway for redemption and restoration.

The message of the cross is not just a historical event; it is the continual unfolding of God's redemptive plan for all humanity. Through the cross, God reveals a love that is patient and longsuffering, a love that is relentless in its pursuit of the lost and unwavering in its desire to bring all creation into harmony with Him. This is a love that transcends the boundaries of time and space, reaching into the depths of human despair, suffering, and even death itself, offering hope where there was none, and light in the darkest of places. As the Apostle Paul writes in Romans 8:38-39: *"For I am persuaded that neither death nor life, nor angels nor principalities nor powers, nor things present nor things to come, nor height nor depth, nor any other created thing, shall be able to separate us from the love of God which is in Christ Jesus our Lord."* This assurance anchors our faith in the unwavering truth that God is love (1 John 4:8,16) and that this love is all-encompassing, never failing, and ever victorious.

In embracing the hope that the cross offers, we are invited to see beyond the immediate struggles of this world to the eternal reality of God's kingdom—a kingdom where love reigns supreme, where justice and mercy meet, and where every tear is wiped away. The witness of the New Testament and the early church fathers shows that the hope of salvation, as offered through the cross, does not end at the grave; it extends into eternity, offering a profound and perhaps even scandalous hope that God's redemptive power is not limited by death (Ephesians 2:7). This is the hope that fuels our faith and gives us courage to face the trials of this life, knowing that the victory has already been won through Christ. The cross assures us that no matter how deep the sin, how profound the loss, or how hopeless the situation, God's love remains steadfast, and His purpose for redemption and restoration will ultimately prevail.

The Promise of Eternal Salvation

As we delve into the eschatological dimensions of the Gospel, we encounter a vision of salvation that is both comprehensive and hopeful. Eternal salvation is not merely a distant promise but a present reality that reshapes our understanding of life and death. The Good News assures us that through Christ, we are not only offered forgiveness but also invited into a relationship that transcends temporal boundaries and ushers us into the eternal embrace of God.

For the wages of sin is death, but the gift of God is eternal life in Christ Jesus our Lord.
Romans 6:23 NKJV

This verse underscores the transformative power of salvation—a gift that not only redeems us from the consequence of sin but also invites us into a life that knows no end. The best translation of eternal life is rendered as the life of the ages to come as seen in N.T. Wright translation; New Testament for Everyone and Bentley Hart's translation.

The promise of eternal salvation is a beacon of hope that guides us through the trials of this present life and assures us of a future beyond the grave. It is a hope that empowers us to live with confidence, purpose, and an unwavering trust in God's ultimate plan.

It is important to warn that Eternal life is not just a future reality; it is a life that we begin to enjoy here and now through our union with Christ. Jesus Himself declares in John 17:3 (NKJV) *"And this is eternal life, that they may know You, the only true God, and Jesus Christ whom You have sent."* This verse emphasizes that eternal life is found in an intimate relationship with God and begins the moment we come to know Him. Apostle John wrote in his first Epistle that eternal life is a present reality.

> *And this is the testimony: that God has given us eternal life, and this life is in His Son.*
> *He who has the Son has life; he who does not have the Son of God does not have life.*
> 1 John 5:11-12 (NKJV)

Here, we see that eternal life is a present possession for those who are in Christ, a transformative reality that shapes our daily existence, filling it with the love, joy, and peace that come from knowing God.

Some of the early church fathers also recognized that eternal life is not merely a distant hope but a present reality. For instance, Augustine, in his work *City of God*, writes, *"Eternal life is the supreme good, and it is in Christ alone that we possess it both now and forever."*(Book 19). He understood that eternal life is intertwined with our current experience of faith, where we begin to partake in the divine nature and live in the light of God's presence. This life is a foretaste of the fullness we will enjoy in the age to come, but it is also the transformative power that renews us in the present, enabling us to live in the victory of Christ even now. Thus, eternal life is both a future promise and a present reality, rooted in our relationship with Christ and experienced through our daily walk with Him. We have Eternal Life now. Hallelujah!

Another early church father Irenaeus of Lyons also affirmed that eternal life is a present reality as well as a future promise. In his seminal work, *Against Heresies*, Irenaeus writes, *"The glory of God is a living man; and the life of man consists in beholding God. But the glory of God is the man fully alive, and the life of man is the vision of God. "* (Book 4, Chapter 20). He emphasized that the experience of eternal life begins here and now as believers encounter the divine life through their relationship with Christ. He believed that the transformative power of God's presence is already active in the lives of Christians, drawing them into a deeper communion with God and transforming their existence. For Irenaeus and the early fathers, eternal life is not just about the future but about the ongoing experience of divine fellowship and transformation in the present age. This perspective aligns with the biblical teaching that eternal life begins with knowing God and living in His light today.

Hope Beyond Death

One of the most profound questions in the human experience is whether there is hope beyond death especially for those who were non-believer when they died. As we explore the theological and biblical perspectives on afterlife and judgment, we are invited to consider the possibility that God's redemptive work extends beyond the confines of this life. The notion of hope beyond death challenges us to rethink traditional understandings of judgment and to embrace a vision of divine justice that is restorative rather than retributive.

For as in Adam all die, even so in Christ all shall be made alive.
1 Corinthians 15:22 KJV

Paul here reflects the inclusive nature of Christ's redemptive work, suggesting that the scope of salvation may reach beyond our current comprehension. This verse captures the essence of Paul's argument about the universal impact of Christ's resurrection and its implications for humanity. By drawing a parallel between the death introduced through Adam and the life offered through Christ, Paul underscores that just as Adam's transgression affected all humanity, so too does Christ's resurrection have the power to reverse this curse and bring life to all. The scope of Christ's redemptive work, as Paul envisions it, suggests that the transformative power of His victory over death is not limited to a select few but is intended for all. This universal aspect of salvation points to the expansive reach of God's grace, which extends beyond the boundaries of the Church and into the wider realm of human existence.

Moreover, this inclusive perspective on salvation highlights the depth of God's mercy and the breadth of His redemptive plan. Paul's assertion implies that the effects of Christ's resurrection have a potential that surpasses mere human understanding. It challenges any notions of a restricted or limited salvation and encourages a vision of divine grace that encompasses the entirety of creation. This inclusive nature of redemption reflects the heart of God's love as revealed through Christ, emphasizing that the promise of new life and restoration is not confined to a specific group but is available to all humanity. The radical nature of this promise invites us to re-evaluate our understanding of salvation and to embrace a hope that extends beyond the immediate and into the eternal, affirming that God's redemptive work in Christ is profoundly inclusive and all-encompassing.

The Victory of God in the Cross

The victory of God, manifested through the cross of Christ, is the central theme that ties together the promise of divine love, eternal salvation, and the hope of redemption beyond death. The cross is not merely a historical event but a cosmic triumph that alters the very fabric of reality. Through Christ's victory over sin, death, and hell, we are offered a glimpse of a new creation—a world where God's justice and mercy reign supreme.

Having disarmed principalities and powers, He made a public spectacle of them, triumphing over them in it.
Colossians 2:15 NKJV

The cross represents a decisive victory over the forces of evil, affirming the ultimate sovereignty of God and the efficacy of His redemptive plan.

In this book, we will journey through the biblical depths and practical implications of these themes, examining how the love of God in Christ and the victory of the cross shape our understanding of salvation and guide us in living out the implications of the Gospel in our daily lives. We will explore the nature of divine justice, the scope of redemption, and the call to live victoriously in the present world, empowered by the hope that Christ's victory brings.

As we embark on this exploration, let us open our hearts to the profound truths of the Gospel and allow them to reshape our lives with the assurance of God's unending love and the hope of eternal salvation. In doing so, we embrace the transformative power of the Good News and live out the victory of Christ in every facet of our existence.

In our exploration of the Gospel's transformative power, it is crucial to address the inclusive scope of divine mercy and its implications for our understanding of hell. Traditional views of hell often emphasize a retributive justice that seems at odds with the all-encompassing love of God revealed in Christ. However, as we delve into a more hopeful and inclusive interpretation, we see that God's mercy and grace extend beyond the limits of human understanding and traditional doctrinal boundaries.

The notion of hell as a place of eternal torment stands in stark contrast to the portrayal of God's love as a redemptive force that seeks to restore rather than simply punish. Scriptural passages such as 1 Timothy 2:4 (*"God desires all men to be saved and to come to the knowledge of the truth"*) and 2 Peter 3:9 (*"The Lord is not slack concerning His promise, as some count slackness, but is longsuffering toward us, not willing that any should perish but that all should come to repentance"*) suggest a divine desire for the ultimate salvation of all humanity. These verses challenge us to consider a perspective of hell that aligns with a God who is relentlessly committed to redeeming every soul.

Moreover, the vision of hell as a place where sin may be finally purged rather than an eternal one allows us to reconcile the concept of divine justice with the notion of restorative love. 1 Corinthians 15:22 that we read earlier assures us that "as in Adam all die, so in Christ all shall be made alive." This inclusive promise of resurrection and restoration underscores a broader scope of salvation that extends beyond immediate judgment. It invites us to envision hell not as an irrevocable destination but as a temporary state where the transformative power of God's love can eventually lead to redemption.

The early church fathers, such as Origen and Gregory of Nyssa, also explored the idea of universal reconciliation and the ultimate victory of God's love over evil. Origen, in his work *De Principiis*, posits that *"the end of all things is the salvation of all,"* reflecting a belief in the ultimate restoration of all creation. This hopeful vision aligns with the scriptural promise that God's grace and mercy are inexhaustible and that His redemptive work will ultimately triumph over all forms of evil and suffering.

By embracing a hopeful, inclusive understanding of hell, we acknowledge that God's love is expansive enough to embrace all of creation, even those who have wandered far from Him. This perspective not only affirms the boundless nature of divine mercy but also inspires us to live out the Gospel with a renewed sense of purpose and hope. It challenges us to view every individual as a recipient of God's grace and to advocate for a vision of salvation that transcends the limitations of traditional doctrines.

As we reflect on the themes of this book, let us be guided by the assurance that God's love, as demonstrated through the cross of Christ, is greater than any darkness we may face. The hope of redemption and the possibility of restoration extend beyond our present understanding, inviting us to trust in the profound mercy of God and to live out our faith with a confidence that His victory will ultimately encompass all of humanity.

Further Reading

1. Augustine of Hippo. *City of God*. Book 19.
2. Irenaeus of Lyons. *Against Heresies*.
3. N.T. Wright. *New Testament for Everyone*.
4. David Bentley Hart. *The New Testament: A Translation*.
5. Origen. *De Principiis*.
6. Gregory of Nyssa. *On the Soul and the Resurrection*.

| 1 |

Judgment and the Nature of God

Eschatology, the study of the last things, has always intrigued and perplexed Christians. Central to this study are questions concerning judgment, hell, and the nature of God. Throughout history, these topics have sparked intense debate, leading to various interpretations and doctrines within the Christian faith. However, to develop a healthy doctrine of last things-eschatology, it is crucial to anchor our understanding in the nature of God as revealed in Jesus Christ—particularly through the event of the cross.

The Cross as the Revelation of God's Nature

The cross is not merely a historical event; it is the ultimate revelation of God's character. The Apostle Paul, in his letter to the Galatians, highlights this central truth:

I am crucified with Christ: nevertheless I live; yet not I, but Christ liveth in me: and the life which I now live in the flesh I live by the faith of the Son of God, who loved me, and gave himself for me
Galatians 2:20, KJV

This verse emphasizes that the Christian life is rooted in Christ's faith and work, not in our efforts. The faithfulness of Christ, who loved us and gave Himself for us, is the foundation upon which our understanding of eschatology must be built. The cross reveals God's self-giving, radically forgiving, and co-suffering love. This love, which is as strong as death (Song of Solomon 8:6), overwhelmed and conquered the powers of Satan, sin, and death. The cross stands as the decisive victory of God over all that opposes His love.

The cross is the fulcrum of God's love and justice, where His holiness and mercy converge in a powerful act of self-sacrifice. Through the cross, we see that God does not remain distant from our suffering but enters fully into it, absorbing our pain, our guilt, and the consequences of our sin. This act is not merely symbolic; it is transformative, breaking down the barriers that separated humanity from God and reconciling us to Him. In Christ's death, every accusation against us is silenced, and every claim of condemnation is defeated, for He bore it all on our behalf. The cross reveals that God's love is not transactional or conditional—it is an unconditional, covenantal love that takes the initiative to rescue and restore. Thus, the cross is the definitive assurance of God's commitment to redeem His creation, providing the foundation for a hopeful eschatology where all things are reconciled in Christ. In light of this, the Christian's hope for the future is not rooted in fear of judgment but in the certainty of God's loving, restorative justice revealed at the cross.

Early Church Father, Athanasius of Alexandria, reflects on this when he writes, "He became what we are so that He might make us what He is." (*On the Incarnation*) Athanasius' words remind us that the cross is not just about the forgiveness of sins but about the transformation of humanity. Through the cross, God entered into our suffering and death to bring us into His life and glory. He summarizes the profound mystery of the Incarnation and the transformative purpose of Christ's work. This phrase, "He became what we are so that He might make us what He is," often cited by theologians, reflects the idea that salvation is not merely about the forgiveness of sins but about the deification (theosis) of humanity.

In this theological vision, Christ did not only assume human nature to restore us from sin but also to elevate humanity into divine life. Athanasius emphasizes that through Christ's suffering, death, and resurrection, men are drawn into the life and glory of God, participating in His divine nature (see 2 Peter 1:4). This participation, sometimes described as the "exchange" between God and humanity, means that the Incarnation enables humanity to share in the life and attributes of God in a mystical and transformative way.

Through the cross, God enters into human suffering to redeem it from within, making it possible for humans not only to be forgiven but also to be renewed and made participants in divine life.

The cross reveals that God's nature is defined not by wrathful vengeance but by self-emptying love. This is embodied in Christ's kenosis, or "self-emptying," as described in Philippians 2:7-8: "He made himself nothing by taking the very nature of a servant, being made in human likeness. And being found in appearance as a man, he humbled himself by becoming obedient to death—even death on a cross!" (NIV). This humility demonstrates that God's power is expressed not through domination but through sacrificial love. As Jürgen Moltmann explains, the suffering God is the One who, in Christ, becomes a companion in our suffering in order to overcome it. He writes, "In the cross of the Son, the grief of the Father is grounded. He suffers the death of his Son in his love for forsaken human beings." Thus, the cross stands as the definitive revelation of God's solidarity with humanity.

This solidarity underscores that divine love seeks not only to restore but to unite humanity with God in a profound relationship. As Hans Urs von Balthasar explained, the cross is the gateway through which we pass into the eternal, self-giving love that defines God's being. This assertion highlights that the crucifixion of Christ is not merely an event of suffering; it is the culmination of God's desire to engage intimately with creation. The cross exemplifies a love that is both sacrificial and transformative, inviting believers to enter into a deeper communion with the divine.

This means that salvation is not merely transactional—an escape from judgment—but relational, drawing believers into the eternal exchange of love within the life of the Trinity. In this view, salvation is understood as a dynamic relationship rather than a one-time event. It emphasizes the ongoing process of becoming one with God, rooted in love and mutual self-giving, which reflects the inner life of the Trinity itself. Through this lens, the cross stands as the bridge between divine and human life, a place where God not only forgives but invites humanity to participate in His eternal love and glory.

This participation is transformative, as it enables believers to share in the divine life, fostering a community of love that echoes the relationship of the Father, Son, and Holy Spirit. The cross, therefore, becomes a symbol of hope and reconciliation, illustrating that through suffering and sacrifice, humanity is drawn closer to God. It is an invitation to live out this relationship in daily life, manifesting God's love to the world and reflecting His glory in the way we relate to others. Ultimately, the cross calls us to embrace our identity as beloved children of God, fully engaged in the divine love that seeks to heal, restore, and unite all of creation.

The Nature of Judgment and Hell in Light of the Cross

When we consider the themes of judgment and hell, it is vital to do so through the lens of the cross. Traditional views often depict judgment as a terrifying event where sinners are cast into eternal conscious torment. However, this view must be re-evaluated in light of God's character as revealed in Jesus.

The cross shows us that God's judgment is not about retribution but about restoration. Jesus Himself declared: *For the Son of man is not come to destroy men's lives, but to save them* (Luke 9:56, KJV). God's judgment is His saving action in the world, aimed at delivering humanity from the powers of sin and death. The early Christians understood this, as evidenced by the writings of Clement of Alexandria. He explained that God does not punish the sinner in order to exact vengeance, but to correct him; and the punishment is for his good, so that he might repent and be saved. Clement's perspective aligns with the biblical view of God's judgment as redemptive rather than punitive. The goal of judgment is not eternal damnation but the restoration of all things in Christ.

The cross further reveals that God's love extends even to those who seem farthest from Him. If Christ's death and resurrection were for all humanity (2 Corinthians 5:14-15), then God's judgment must reflect His desire for reconciliation rather than exclusion. This aligns with N.T. Wright's assertion that God's purpose is always restorative. He submitted that the point of the biblical story is that God's justice is aimed at putting the world to rights, not at punishing for the sake of it. Hell, seen through this lens, is not merely a place of torment but a state of alienation from God's love. Yet even in this state, hope remains, for His mercy endures forever (Psalm 136:1), suggesting that no one is ever beyond the reach of God's love.

This perspective invites us to rethink judgment and hell as part of God's redemptive work in restoring creation to Himself. T.F. Torrance emphasizes that the wrath of God must be understood as the fire of His love for the sinner, a fire that consumes sin but not the sinner (*Incarnation: The Person and Life of Christ pg. 249-256*). Hell, in this view, is not a permanent rejection but a purifying process where God's love confronts resistance to His will. As such, judgment is not the end of hope but the beginning of renewal, pointing toward the time when all things will be summed up in Christ (Ephesians 1:10).

Hell: A Biblical and Historical Perspective

The concept of hell has also been the subject of much debate. Traditional views often depict hell as a place of eternal conscious torment. However, this interpretation is not the only one within

Christian history. The early church held a more nuanced view of hell, seeing it as a place of purification rather than eternal punishment.

Origen of Alexandria expressed a view of hell that emphasized God's purifying love: *The consuming fire is not a material thing, but the fire of conscience, which consumes sin and restores man to his true nature.* (De Principiis, Book 2). This understanding of hell as a process of purification rather than eternal torment reflects a broader patristic consensus. Many early theologians saw hell as a temporary state where souls are purified and eventually restored to communion with God.

In more contemporary times, theologians like Hans Urs von Balthasar have also emphasized the hope that all might be saved: *We are allowed to hope that no human being ever reaches the point of final damnation because the infinite love of God can always find ways to bring the stray sheep back into the fold.* (Dare We Hope "That All Men Be Saved"?) Balthasar's hope is rooted in the boundless love and mercy of God, revealed in Jesus Christ. This perspective invites us to rethink the traditional doctrine of hell in light of God's redemptive purpose for all creation.

The Eschatological Victory of Christ

It is important at this time to note that at the heart of eschatology is the victory of Christ over death, Hades, and hell. The New Testament presents this victory as the central event in the history of salvation. The Apostle Paul proclaims: Forasmuch then as the children are partakers of flesh and blood, he also himself likewise took part of the same; that through death he might destroy him that had the power of death, that is, the devil, Hebrews 2:14, KJV. Christ's victory over death is not just a future hope but a present reality. Through His death and resurrection, Christ has defeated the powers of darkness and opened the way for all humanity to share in His victory. This is powerfully expressed in the early Christian hymn:

Christ is risen from the dead,
Trampling down death by death,
And upon those in the tombs
Bestowing life.
Paschal Troparion, Eastern Orthodox Church

This hymn, sung during the Pascha (Easter) celebration, encapsulates the triumph of Christ over death. It is a reminder that the ultimate outcome of history is not destruction but life—life in the fullness of God's kingdom. The victory of Christ is also depicted in the Book of Revelation, where Jesus declares: I am he that liveth, and was dead; and, behold, I am alive for evermore, Amen; and have the keys of hell and of death Revelation 1:18, KJV. Christ's possession of the keys of hell and death signifies His absolute authority over them. Hell and death are no longer realms of fear for the believer; they are conquered territories, subject to the Lordship of Christ.

If one is to have a healthy understanding of eschatology, it has to be rooted in the revelation of God's love and victory through the cross of Christ. It views judgment and hell through the lens of God's redemptive purpose and emphasizes the ultimate victory of Christ over all powers of darkness. This eschatology is not about fear but about hope—hope in the God who has triumphed over death and offers life to all who believe in Him.

Further Reading

1. Athanasius of Alexandria, *On the Incarnation*
2. Clement of Alexandria, *Stromata*, Book 7
3. Origen of Alexandria, *De Principiis*, Book 2
4. Moltmann, Jürgen. *The Crucified God: The Cross of Christ as the Foundation and Criticism of Christian Theology*. Fortress Press, 1993.
   Moltmann, Jürgen. *Theology of Hope: On the Ground and the Implications of a Christian Eschatology*. Harper & Row, 1967.

5. Balthasar, Hans Urs von. *Mysterium Paschale: The Mystery of Easter*. Translated by Andrew Louth. Ignatius Press, 1990. Balthasar, Hans Urs von. *Dare We Hope "That All Men Be Saved"?* Ignatius Press, 1988.

6. N.T. Wright, *Surprised by Hope*

7. Torrance, Thomas F. *Incarnation: The Person and Life of Christ*. InterVarsity Press, 2008.

8. *Paschal Troparion*, Eastern Orthodox Church

| 2 |

Christ's Victory Over Death, Hades, and Hell

In the study of eschatology, understanding how early Christians interpreted the Old Testament through the lens of Christ's resurrection is crucial. The resurrection of Jesus was not merely a miraculous event; it was a profound revelation that reshaped the understanding of Scripture and its promises. Deeply impacted by this transformative event, early Christians began to read the Old Testament with a renewed perspective, recognizing that the entire narrative of salvation history culminated in the person of Jesus Christ.

This christological interpretation is foundational for comprehending how the early Church viewed Christ's victory over death, Hades, and hell. After His resurrection, Jesus clarified this reinterpretation to His disciples. In Luke 24:44-47, He explained that everything written about Him in the Law of Moses, the Prophets, and the Psalms had been fulfilled. His suffering, death, and resurrection were not isolated events but integral to the divine plan revealed throughout the Old Testament. This teaching underscores a pivotal shift: what was once seen as mere prophetic anticipation is now recognized as fulfilled reality in Christ.

Jesus' post-resurrection appearances were characterized by this revelatory teaching. For instance, on the road to Emmaus, He expounded on the Scriptures, showing how they pointed to Himself

(Luke 24:27). This moment of enlightenment was not just a historical account but a theological cornerstone, establishing that Christ's victory was anticipated and foretold throughout the Hebrew Scriptures.

Early Christian writers and Church Fathers reflected this interpretive approach. The apostle Paul, in 1 Corinthians 15:54-57, exulted in Christ's triumph over death, saying, *"Death is swallowed up in victory. O Death, where is your victory? O Death, where is your sting?"* This victory is not merely a future hope but a present reality for believers, illustrating that Christ's resurrection fundamentally altered the status of death and hell. Paul's assertion that *"the sting of death is sin, and the power of sin is the law"* is followed by the profound declaration, *"thanks be to God, who gives us the victory through our Lord Jesus Christ."*

The early Church Fathers expanded upon this victory. Origen, in his work *On First Principles*, emphasized the cosmic significance of Christ's resurrection, stating that it not only secured salvation for humanity but also restored creation itself. He articulated that through Christ, death was rendered powerless, aligning with the prophetic assurances found in the Old Testament.

Similarly, Irenaeus emphasized that Christ's resurrection decisively defeated the powers of darkness and death that had held humanity captive. He argued that Jesus' victory was not merely symbolic but a real and effective conquest over the forces of evil. Athanasius, in *On the Incarnation*, affirmed that Christ's death and resurrection dismantled the stronghold of death and liberated those bound by it.

This theological framework had practical implications for early Christians' understanding of salvation and the afterlife. The belief in Christ's victory over death, Hades, and hell provided hope and assurance in the face of suffering and mortality. It was a transformative doctrine that redefined their expectations of God's redemptive plan and the ultimate destiny of humanity.

As we delve deeper into the implications of Christ's victory, it becomes clear that the resurrection is not merely a miraculous event but the cornerstone of Christian eschatological hope. It reshapes our understanding of death, hell, and the promise of eternal life, affirming that the defeat of these forces is both a present reality and a future expectation. Through Christ's victory, we are invited into a new relationship with God, marked by hope, renewal, and the assurance of ultimate redemption.

Again, it is crucial to understand how early Christians read the Old Testament in light of Christ's resurrection. After the resurrection, they began to interpret the Scriptures christologically, seeing all promises and prophecies fulfilled in Him. This is evident from Jesus' teaching:

> *Ought not Christ to have suffered these things, and to enter into his glory? And beginning at Moses and all the prophets, he expounded unto them in all the scriptures the things concerning himself.*
> Luke 24:26-27, KJV

The Apostle Paul emphasized this transformation in understanding:

> *But their minds were blinded: for until this day remaineth the same vail untaken away in the reading of the old testament; which vail is done aways in Christ... But we all, with open face beholding as in a glass the glory of the Lord, are changed into the same image from glory to glory, even as by the Spirit of the Lord.*
> 2 Corinthians 3:14, 18, KJV

Let's explore some key Old Testament passages interpreted christologically by the early church:

Song of Solomon 8:6

> *Set me as a seal upon thine heart, as a seal upon thine arm: for love is strong as death; jealousy is cruel as the grave: the coals thereof are coals of fire, which hath a most vehement flame.*

Song of Solomon 8:6, KJV

In Song of Solomon 8:6, the verse speaks powerfully about love by comparing it to death and jealousy. Love is described as being "strong as death," suggesting that true love is unbreakable and can endure anything, even the hardest trials. Death, which seems final and powerful, cannot overcome genuine love. The verse also mentions jealousy as "cruel as the grave," reminding us that jealousy can lead to pain and suffering. This contrasts with the beauty of love, which, while intense, brings joy and connection between people. In this poetic imagery, we see how love has the power to overcome even the darkest of circumstances.

Early Christians understood this verse in a deeper way by connecting it to the love of Christ. They believed that Christ's love is stronger than death itself, as His resurrection defeated death and sin. Just as the verse talks about love being a seal on the heart, early believers saw Christ's love as a mark on their hearts, showing their commitment to Him. They believed that His love could conquer even the flames of Hades, the place of the dead. This interpretation highlights the hope and assurance found in Christ's love, which is eternal and unshakeable, offering comfort and strength to those who believe in Him. In this way, the Song of Solomon becomes not just a celebration of romantic love but also a powerful testimony to the greater love that Christ has for humanity.

Psalm 107:10-16

Such as sit in darkness and in the shadow of death, being bound in affliction and iron; Because they rebelled against the words of God, and contemned the counsel of the most High: Therefore he brought down their heart with labour; they fell down, and there was none to help. Then they cried unto the LORD in their trouble, and he saved them out of their distresses. He brought them out of darkness and the shadow of death, and

brake their bands in sunder. Oh that men would praise the LORD for his goodness, and for his wonderful works to the children of men! For he hath broken the gates of brass, and cut the bars of iron in sunder.
Psalm 107:10-16, KJV

Psalm 107:10-16 describes a powerful transformation from darkness to light, capturing the plight of those who find themselves trapped in despair and suffering. The verses begin by illustrating the deep anguish of those "sitting in darkness" and "in the shadow of death," bound by affliction. This imagery evokes a sense of hopelessness, as these individuals are described as having rebelled against God, which led them to this state of bondage. Their rebellion resulted in a heavy heart, and when they realized their dire situation, they cried out to the Lord for help. This moment of desperation highlights the human condition—often finding ourselves in dark places, we can turn to God in our troubles.

The Psalm shifts dramatically as it reveals God's response to their cries. He rescues them from their distress, bringing them out of darkness and breaking the chains that bind them. This liberation is reminiscent of Christ's mission to free those held captive by sin and death. Early Christians saw parallels between this Psalm and Christ's descent into Hades, where He proclaimed victory and released the souls who had been waiting in darkness. The concluding verses call for praise for God's goodness and His wonderful works, emphasizing the joy and gratitude that should arise from recognizing His power to break the chains of sin and death. Thus, this Psalm serves not only as a reflection of individual suffering and redemption but also as a prophetic glimpse into the greater victory achieved through Christ's death and resurrection.

Psalm 24:7-10

> *Lift up your heads, O ye gates; and be ye lift up, ye everlasting doors;*
> *and the King of glory shall come in. Who is this King of glory? The*
> *LORD strong and mighty, the LORD mighty in battle. Lift up your*
> *heads, O ye gates; even lift them up, ye everlasting doors; and the King of*
> *glory shall come in. Who is this King of glory? The LORD of hosts, he is*
> *the King of glory. Selah.*
>
> Psalm 24:7-10, KJV

Psalm 24:7-10 presents a powerful and poetic invitation for the gates and doors to lift up, heralding the arrival of the "King of glory." This call serves as a proclamation of the majesty and sovereignty of God, emphasizing His strength and authority over all creation. The repeated phrase "lift up your heads" creates a sense of urgency and expectation, as if the very structures of the earth are being beckoned to recognize the arrival of divine royalty. The question "Who is this King of glory?" is posed to evoke contemplation and awe, leading the audience to reflect on the nature and identity of God. The psalmist answers this question by declaring that the King of glory is "the LORD strong and mighty," emphasizing that God's power and might are unparalleled.

The imagery within these verses also carries a deeper significance regarding the nature of God's relationship with humanity. The "everlasting doors" symbolize not only barriers but also the idea of permanence and eternity. By commanding these doors to lift, the psalm emphasizes that God's glory is not confined or restricted; instead, it breaks through barriers, signifying His dominion over all realms, including the spiritual. The repetition of the call to lift up the gates reinforces the importance of recognizing and welcoming God's presence. It serves as a reminder that God, as the mighty warrior, is actively involved in the affairs of the world and is worthy of honor and reverence.

In the Eastern Orthodox tradition, this Psalm is particularly significant during the Pascha (Easter) service, where it symbolizes Christ's triumphant entry into Hades. The understanding of the "everlasting doors" as the gates of Hades serves to illustrate Christ's victory over death. By entering Hades, Christ demonstrates His authority over the realm of the dead, liberating those held captive and affirming that death does not have the final say. This interpretation enriches the psalm's meaning, portraying Christ not only as the King of glory but also as the one who conquers darkness and death. Thus, Psalm 24:7-10 encapsulates the essence of God's victorious nature and His commitment to redeeming humanity, reinforcing the message of hope and triumph that resonates throughout the biblical narrative.

Isaiah 25:6-9

> *And in this mountain shall the LORD of hosts make unto all people a feast of fat things, a feast of wines on the lees, of fat things full of marrow, of wines on the lees well refined. And he will destroy in this mountain the face of the covering cast over all people, and the vail that is spread over all nations. He will swallow up death in victory; and the Lord GOD will wipe away tears from off all faces; and the rebuke of his people shall he take away from off all the earth: for the LORD hath spoken it. And it shall be said in that day, Lo, this is our God; we have waited for him, and he will save us: this is the LORD; we have waited for him, we will be glad and rejoice in his salvation.* Isaiah 25:6-9, KJV

Isaiah 25:6-9 paints a vivid picture of a divine celebration on Mount Zion, characterized by abundance and joy. The imagery of a feast filled with "fat things" and "wines on the lees" signifies the richness of God's blessings and His generosity towards humanity. This banquet is not merely for a select few; it is described as being for "all people," highlighting God's inclusive nature and His desire to bring everyone into His fold. The use of lavish imagery evokes a sense of festivity and hope, indicating that God's ultimate plan involves a joyful restoration of creation, where His people can partake in His goodness.

Central to this passage is the promise of God's victory over death. The declaration that He "will swallow up death in victory" emphasizes the transformative power of God's intervention in the world. This act signifies not just the end of physical death, but also the obliteration of the spiritual separation that sin brings. By destroying the "face of the covering cast over all people" and the "vail that is spread over all nations," God is revealing His truth and presence to all humanity, dismantling the barriers that keep people from experiencing His love and salvation. This imagery reassures believers that God's redemptive work will ultimately triumph over despair and darkness.

The concluding verses reflect the joyous response of God's people to His salvation. The exclamation "Lo, this is our God; we have waited for him" signifies a culmination of hope and anticipation, reinforcing the faithfulness of God to His promises. The repetition of the phrase "we will be glad and rejoice in his salvation" expresses an overwhelming sense of gratitude and celebration for the deliverance God provides. Early Christians interpreted this passage as a foreshadowing of Christ's victory through His resurrection, recognizing that in Him, the fullness of this prophecy finds its fulfillment. The promise of a future where tears are wiped away and rebuke is removed serves as a powerful source of hope, affirming that God's ultimate intention is to bring restoration and joy to His creation.

Zechariah 9:11

> *As for thee also, by the blood of thy covenant I have sent forth thy*
> *prisoners out of the pit wherein is no water.*
> Zechariah 9:11, KJV

Zechariah 9:11 presents a powerful image of deliverance and hope through the metaphor of a covenant. The phrase "by the blood of thy covenant" signifies a sacred agreement established between God and

His people, where the shedding of blood represents sacrifice and redemption. In the context of the New Testament, this blood is understood to refer to the sacrificial death of Jesus Christ, who fulfilled the requirements of the old covenant and instituted a new covenant of grace. This transformative act of love not only reconciles humanity to God but also establishes a means of salvation for all who believe.

The reference to sending forth "thy prisoners out of the pit wherein is no water" paints a vivid picture of liberation. The "pit" symbolizes a place of desolation and despair, much like Hades in early Christian thought, where souls were held captive. In this passage, God promises to rescue those imprisoned in such a state, highlighting His compassion and commitment to restore those who are lost. The imagery of a pit without water evokes feelings of hopelessness and thirst, representing the spiritual emptiness that comes from separation from God. By sending forth these prisoners, God demonstrates His authority over death and His desire to bring about spiritual renewal.

Early Christians interpreted this passage as prophetic of Christ's mission to deliver souls from Hades. Just as God promised to rescue the prisoners in Zechariah's time, Christ's death and resurrection accomplished this deliverance on a cosmic scale. Through His blood, humanity is set free from the bondage of sin and death, receiving the promise of eternal life. This understanding emphasizes not only the efficacy of Christ's sacrifice but also reassures us that through Him, we have access to the living water that satisfies the deepest longings of our souls, offering hope and joy in the face of despair.

* * *

The New Testament writers continue this theme of Christ's victory over death and Hades, offering further testimony to His triumph. They also looked into the promises in the Old Testament and examined the incarnation, life, death, and burial, including the ascension. Let us see a few of their witnesses.

Ephesians 4:8-10

> *Wherefore he saith, When he ascended up on high, he led captivity captive, and gave gifts unto men. (Now that he ascended, what is it but that he also descended first into the lower parts of the earth? He that descended is the same also that ascended up far above all heavens, that he might fill all things.)*
> Ephesians 4:8-10, KJV

Ephesians 4:8-10 presents a profound theological insight into the work of Christ and His redemptive mission. The phrase "When he ascended up on high, he led captivity captive" signifies the victorious nature of Christ's resurrection and ascension. In this context, "captivity" refers to those held captive by sin and death, particularly the souls in Hades who were awaiting salvation. Christ's ascension is depicted as a triumphant victory march, where He not only conquers death but also liberates those who were in spiritual bondage, bringing them into the fullness of life and salvation.

The passage also emphasizes the dual aspect of Christ's journey: His descent before His ascent. The mention of Christ "descending into the lower parts of the earth" is interpreted as His descent into Hades or the realm of the dead. This act is significant because it shows that Christ entered into the depths of human experience, even confronting death itself. By doing so, He demonstrated His authority over all realms, including the grave. This descent was not a sign of defeat but a necessary step in His mission to reclaim and restore humanity, emphasizing that He fully understands and engages with the human condition.

Finally, the concluding statement, "that he might fill all things," encapsulates the purpose of Christ's work. His resurrection and ascension lead to the fulfillment of God's plan for creation, where Christ reigns supreme over all. Through His victory, He bestows gifts upon His followers, empowering them for service and ministry. This passage affirms the hope that believers can have in Christ's authority and the assurance that through His death and resurrection, they are liberated from the bondage of sin and given new life, enabling them to participate in the fullness of His kingdom.

Revelation 1:18

I am he that liveth, and was dead; and, behold, I am alive for evermore, Amen; and have the keys of hell and of death.
Revelation 1:18, KJV

Revelation 1:18 presents a powerful proclamation from Jesus, affirming His eternal nature and victory over death. When He declared, "I am he that liveth, and was dead; and, behold, I am alive for evermore," Jesus underscores the significance of His resurrection. This declaration not only emphasizes His triumph over physical death but also signifies His divine authority as the risen Lord. By declaring that He holds "the keys of hell and of death," Jesus asserts His dominion over the realms of death and the afterlife, ensuring that no power can prevail against Him. This reinforces the central Christian belief that, through His resurrection, death is defeated and eternal life is offered to all. Those who believe in Him will experience this life now and forever.

The early church recognized the profound implications of Christ's resurrection for humanity and the cosmos. They understood it as the pivotal event in God's redemptive plan, marking a new beginning for creation itself. Christ's victory over death not only assures individual believers of their future resurrection but also initiates a broader cosmic transformation. This transformative power is echoed in Romans 8:19-21, where Paul describes creation itself eagerly waiting for the revelation of the children of God. The resurrection serves as the firstfruits of this renewal, signaling that the brokenness of the world will one day be restored, culminating in a new heaven and a new earth where death and sorrow will be no more.

Ultimately, Revelation 1:18 encapsulates the hope and assurance that the early Christians found in the resurrection of Christ. They believed that through His death and resurrection, Jesus had secured a definitive victory, not only for themselves but for all of creation. This message of hope continues to resonate today, reminding believers that because Christ lives, they too will live, and that His authority over hell and death guarantees their eternal security in Him. The promise of resurrection is not merely a future event but a present reality that empowers believers to live in the light of His victory, transforming their lives and the world around them.

1 Peter 3:18-20

The apostle Peter offers a compelling perspective on Christ's victory in his epistle:

> *For Christ also hath once suffered for sins, the just for the unjust, that he might bring us to God, being put to death in the flesh, but quickened by the Spirit: By which also he went and preached unto the spirits in prison; which sometime were disobedient, when once the longsuffering of God waited in the days of Noah, while the ark was a-preparing, wherein few, that is, eight souls were saved by water.*
> 1 Peter 3:18-20, KJV

In 1 Peter 3:18-20, the apostle Peter provides a profound insight into the significance of Christ's suffering and subsequent victory. He writes, "For Christ also hath once suffered for sins, the just for the unjust, that he might bring us to God." This statement highlights the redemptive purpose of Christ's sacrifice, emphasizing that His death was not just a tragic event but a pivotal act of love intended to reconcile humanity with God. Peter further elaborates that Christ, after His death, was "quickened by the Spirit," indicating that He was made alive and empowered to accomplish further purposes beyond the grave.

One of the most striking elements of this passage is the assertion that Christ "went and preached unto the spirits in prison." This phrase suggests that even after His death, Jesus reached out to those who had been disobedient in the past, specifically referencing the time of Noah. This act demonstrates Christ's authority over death and Hades, affirming that His redemptive work extends beyond earthly life. The early church interpreted this as a powerful testament to the victory of Christ, as it implied that no one is beyond the reach of His grace—even those who had died in their sins. Peter's words introduce a glimmer of hope, indicating that there may still be opportunities for redemption after death.

This understanding resonates deeply with the belief that God's mercy is expansive and enduring. By highlighting Christ's ability to reach even those who had previously rejected Him, Peter opens the door to the possibility of hope after death. This notion would have provided comfort to early Christians facing persecution and uncertainty, reinforcing their faith in a God who desires to bring all to salvation. The passage not only emphasizes the victory of Christ over sin and death but also serves as a reminder that His love and grace extend beyond the grave, inviting all to partake in the hope of eternal life.

* * *

The resurrection of Jesus is the linchpin of Christian eschatology. Early Christians, through a christological lens, reinterpreted the Old Testament, unveiling the truth that all scriptural promises find their fulfillment in Christ. This reinterpretation transformed their understanding of death, hell, and salvation, offering profound hope for a future resurrection and eternal life. The early Church's theological reflections illustrate that Christ's victory over death is not only a historical event but a present reality, inviting all believers into a renewed relationship with God and the assurance of ultimate redemption.

The early church fathers echoed and expanded upon these scriptural testimonies, emphasizing the victory of Christ over death, Hades, and hell. Ignatius of Antioch, in his letter to the Ephesians, reflects on Christ's triumph: *He descended into Hades alone, but He arose accompanied by a multitude.* Ignatius highlights the communal aspect of Christ's victory—He did not rise alone, but brought with Him those who had been held captive.

Clement of Alexandria also speaks of Christ's descent into Hades as an act of divine love: *The Lord preached the gospel to those in Hades...that all who would believe might be saved.* Clement's understanding of Christ's descent into Hades as a mission of salvation aligns with the broader early Christian belief that Christ's victory extended to all, even the dead, and of course the dead not just spiritual.

Finally, Origen indeed elaborates on the purifying aspect of Christ's victory: *The fire of judgment is not a material fire, but the fire of divine love that purges sin and restores the soul to its original purity.* For Origen, Christ's victory over death and hell is not about punishment, but about purification and restoration—a theme that would resonate throughout Christian history.

As we wrap up this chapter, we remember how we have explored how the early Christians, through a christological reading of the Old Testament, understood the victory of Christ over death, Hades, and hell. This victory is central to a healthy eschatology, offering hope and assurance of the ultimate triumph of life over death, love over fear, and Christ over all the powers of darkness.

In this next chapter, we will look at more scriptural evidence of the victory of the cross of Christ and its implications for now and hereafter.

Further Reading

1. Ignatius of Antioch, *Epistle to the Ephesians*, Chapter 19
2. Clement of Alexandria, *Stromata*, Book 6, Chapter 6
3. Origen, *De Principiis*, Book 2, Chapter 10

| 3 |

Christ's Victory Foretold

Just as we have seen in the previous chapter, the Old Testament contains numerous prophecies and passages that early Christians interpreted as foretelling Christ's victory over death, hell, and the forces of darkness. These scriptures were not only seen as prophetic markers pointing to Christ's life, death, and resurrection but also as theological insights into God's redemptive plan for humanity

Early Christians, particularly in the writings of the apostles and Church Fathers, approached these texts with a Christocentric lens, believing that the promises and prophecies found in the Old Testament were fulfilled in the person and work of Jesus. They saw the resurrection not as an isolated miracle but as the culmination of God's purpose, long anticipated in Israel's scriptures. For example, passages about deliverance from Sheol (the realm of the dead), triumph over enemies, and the restoration of life were read as foreshadowing Christ's victory over sin, death, and hell.

This interpretive approach, known as typology, identified patterns and figures—such as Jonah's three days in the belly of the fish, or the sacrificial system in Leviticus—as types that found their ultimate meaning in Christ. Additionally, Psalms and prophetic books like Isaiah, Ezekiel, and Hosea contained language that was reinterpreted in light of the resurrection.

We will explore some of these key scriptures in this work, highlighting how early Christians saw them as more than mere historical accounts or poetic expressions. Instead, they viewed them as part of a divine narrative that anticipated Christ's descent into death and His subsequent resurrection, which defeated death and opened the way to eternal life. We will in this chapter continue to delve deeper into these Old Testament texts, examining both their original context and how the New Testament writers and early theologians understood them. This exploration will further illuminate how the resurrection was not an unexpected event but the fulfillment of ancient hopes and prophecies embedded within the Hebrew scriptures.

Psalm 16:10

> *For thou wilt not leave my soul in hell; neither wilt thou suffer thine*
> *Holy One to see corruption."*
> Psalm 16:10, KJV

This verse is central to the Christian understanding of Christ's resurrection. Peter quotes it in his Pentecost sermon in Acts 2:27, explaining that David spoke of the resurrection of Christ, who was not abandoned to Hades, nor did His flesh see corruption. This prophecy is a clear foretelling of Christ's triumph over death, ensuring that He would not be left in the grave.

Psalm 16:10 expresses a profound theological truth about God's power over death and His promise of preservation. While David originally spoke these words, early Christians understood that they found their ultimate fulfillment in Christ. The reference to the "soul" not being left in "hell" (or *Sheol*, the realm of the dead) signifies more than just escape from physical death; it points to complete victory over the forces of sin, death, and separation from God. Christ's resurrection demonstrates not merely survival after death but the undoing of death itself, marking the dawn of new creation.

Moreover, the phrase "neither wilt thou suffer thine Holy One to see corruption" emphasizes that Christ's body did not undergo decay, underscoring the miraculous nature of His resurrection. Unlike others who are subject to the normal process of bodily decomposition, Christ's resurrection was immediate and triumphant. This unique preservation signifies the holiness and divine nature of Jesus, showing that death had no rightful claim over Him. For believers, this verse also offers hope: just as Christ was not abandoned to corruption, those who are united with Him by faith can trust in the promise of their own resurrection and the assurance of eternal life in God's presence.

Isaiah 26:19

Thy dead men shall live, together with my dead body shall they arise. Awake and sing, ye that dwell in dust: for thy dew is as the dew of herbs, and the earth shall cast out the dead.
Isaiah 26:19, KJV

Isaiah's prophecy of the resurrection is seen as a foreshadowing of Christ's resurrection and the general resurrection of the dead. The phrase "together with my dead body shall they arise" is understood as a reference to Christ leading the faithful out of death and into eternal life.

Isaiah 26:19 presents a powerful image of hope and renewal, affirming that death is not the end. The phrase "thy dead men shall live" reflects the expectation of bodily resurrection, not just spiritual survival. This prophecy points beyond mere restoration to a new reality where life triumphs over death, anticipating the resurrection through Christ. His victory ensures that those united with Him will also rise, breaking the power of death. The call to "awake and sing" encourages joyful expectation, symbolizing the transformation from death to life as an occasion of celebration.

The imagery of "dew" in this verse conveys the idea of refreshment and renewal, much like how morning dew restores vegetation. In a similar way, God's life-giving power will revive those who "dwell in the dust," bringing them back to life. The phrase "the earth shall cast out the dead" emphasizes the inevitability of resurrection, with creation itself yielding to God's power. For Christians, this prophecy not only reflects Christ's resurrection but also affirms the hope of the future resurrection, when all who belong to Him will rise and share in the fullness of eternal life.

Ezekiel 37:12-14

Therefore prophesy and say unto them, Thus saith the Lord GOD; Behold, O my people, I will open your graves, and cause you to come up out of your graves, and bring you into the land of Israel. And ye shall know that I am the LORD, when I have opened your graves, O my people, and brought you up out of your graves, And shall put my spirit in you, and ye shall live, and I shall place you in your own land: then shall ye know that I the LORD have spoken it, and performed it, saith the LORD.
Ezekiel 37:12-14, KJV

The vision of the dry bones in Ezekiel is another prophetic image of resurrection, which the early church fathers saw as symbolizing the resurrection brought by Christ. The opening of graves and the imparting of the Spirit reflect the new life that Christ grants to believers through His resurrection.

Ezekiel 37:12-14 presents a striking image of renewal, restoration, and resurrection. The promise to "open your graves" and "cause you to come up" not only addresses the immediate context of Israel's return from exile but also points to a deeper, eschatological reality. This prophetic act signifies God's power to reverse death and restore life, prefiguring the resurrection of Christ, who opens the grave for all believers. The restoration to the land symbolizes more than geographical return; it represents spiritual renewal and participation in God's covenant blessings.

The imparting of God's Spirit in this prophecy emphasizes that resurrection is not merely physical but involves a complete transformation of life through divine empowerment. This aligns with the Christian understanding of the Holy Spirit's work in believers, who are made alive in Christ through His resurrection. Just as God breathed life into Adam, the Spirit breathes new life into those who were spiritually and physically dead, bringing them into the fullness of life. For Christians, this vision reinforces the hope of both present spiritual regeneration and the future bodily resurrection at the end of time.

Hosea 13:14

I will ransom them from the power of the grave; I will redeem them from death: O death, I will be thy plagues; O grave, I will be thy destruction: repentance shall be hid from mine eyes.
Hosea 13:14, KJV

This verse from Hosea is a powerful declaration of God's intention to defeat death and redeem His people from the grave. The Apostle Paul echoes this passage in 1 Corinthians 15:55, celebrating Christ's victory over death and the grave. The early church viewed this as a prophecy of the defeat of death through Christ's resurrection.

Hosea's prophecy is not merely about deliverance from physical death but symbolizes God's ultimate power to reverse the curse of mortality and restore life. The use of the terms "plagues" and "destruction" toward death reflects a deliberate reversal—death, which once plagued humanity, will now itself be plagued and destroyed. This points toward the idea that death's dominion is not eternal but subject to God's redemptive plan. God's promise to ransom His people from the grave emphasizes His unwavering intention to restore life and triumph over all forms of death and separation.

The fact that "repentance shall be hid from mine eyes" further reinforces the certainty and irreversibility of God's victory. There will be no change or reconsideration of His redemptive purpose. This verse finds its ultimate fulfillment in Christ's resurrection, where death is rendered powerless and believers are assured of eternal life.

For early Christians, Hosea's words encapsulated the heart of the Gospel—the death and resurrection of Christ signaled not only the defeat of physical death but also the promise of new, everlasting life for all who trust in Him.

Job 19:25-27

For I know that my redeemer liveth, and that he shall stand at the latter day upon the earth: And though after my skin worms destroy this body, yet in my flesh shall I see God: Whom I shall see for myself, and mine eyes shall behold, and not another; though my reins be consumed within me.
Job 19:25-27, KJV

Job's declaration of faith in a living Redeemer who will stand upon the earth and raise him from the dead is one of the clearest Old Testament testimonies to the hope of resurrection. Early Christians saw this as a prophetic reference to Christ's resurrection and the ultimate resurrection of the faithful.

Job expresses an unshakeable conviction that even though his body will perish, he will one day be restored to see God with his own eyes. This reflects a profound belief in bodily resurrection, where the individual will be physically reunited with God. The statement that his "Redeemer lives" suggests a hope that transcends death, pointing to a divine figure who will act decisively to vindicate and restore him. For Christians, this Redeemer is Christ, who not only stands as the advocate for humanity but also guarantees the resurrection through His own triumph over death.

The personal nature of Job's hope—"Whom I shall see for myself, and mine eyes shall behold"—underscores the intimate relationship between God and His redeemed people. This aligns with the Christian teaching that believers will not merely survive death in a disembodied state but will experience a bodily resurrection to be with God eternally. The phrase "though my reins be consumed within me" conveys that even amid physical decay, Job's hope remains intact, symbolizing the transformative power of resurrection. Early church interpretations emphasized that Christ's resurrection inaugurated this hope, assuring believers that they, too, will see God face to face in the resurrection.

* * *

The Old Testament is filled with prophecies and imagery that point toward the triumph over death and the promise of new life. These passages reflect God's intention to redeem His people, not just spiritually, but through a bodily resurrection that restores creation. For the early Christian community, the resurrection of Christ was the fulfillment of these ancient promises. His victory over death was not an isolated event but the culmination of God's plan foretold throughout Scripture, demonstrating that life and restoration have the final word.

The New Testament writers, also inspired by the Holy Spirit, drew on many Old Testament prophecies to articulate the victory of Christ over death and Hades. They recognized in Christ's resurrection the fulfillment of God's promises to overcome the grave, and they wove these themes into their teachings. Here are key passages that reflect this understanding:

Matthew 16:18

> *And I say also unto thee, That thou art Peter, and upon this rock I will build my church; and the gates of hell shall not prevail against it.*
> Matthew 16:18, KJV

In this declaration, Jesus affirms the strength and resilience of His church, with the promise that the gates of hell (Hades) will not prevail against it. This passage has been interpreted as a confirmation of Christ's ultimate victory over death and the forces of hell, ensuring that His church will endure.

The "gates of hell" symbolize the power of death and the realm of the dead, which held humanity in bondage before Christ's resurrection. By stating that these gates will not prevail, Jesus foretells His triumph over death, accomplished through His death and resurrection. Christ's victory broke the power of death, releasing all who were under its dominion. This ensures that the church, as the community of believers united with the resurrected Christ, shares in that victory and stands secure against every threat, including death itself.

Moreover, this statement points to the ongoing mission of the church. Empowered by Christ's resurrection and the indwelling Holy Spirit, the church is not a passive entity but an advancing force. The imagery of "gates" suggests that it is the gates of Hades under siege—not the church. Through the proclamation of the Gospel, the church actively participates in extending Christ's victory over sin, death, and spiritual darkness. This guarantees that not even death can extinguish the life Christ has imparted to His people. That is why we must learn the right Gospel and how to preach the good news: the good news is that Christ has included us in the victory He won for us. The Gospel is not that we give our lives to Christ, but that Christ gave His life to us. The Gospel is not that we receive Him, but that He has received us into the circle of love. Knowing and acknowledging this will transform our lives.

1 Corinthians 15:20-26

But now is Christ risen from the dead, and become the firstfruits of them that slept. For since by man came death, by man came also the resurrection of the dead. For as in Adam all die, even so in Christ shall all be made alive. But every man in his own order: Christ the firstfruits; afterward they that are Christ's at his coming. Then cometh the end, when he shall have delivered up the kingdom to God, even the Father; when he shall have put down all rule and all authority and power. For he must reign, till he hath put all enemies under his feet. The last enemy that shall be destroyed is death.
1 Corinthians 15:20-26, KJV

Paul's first letter to the Corinthians contains one of the most detailed expositions of the resurrection. Christ is the "firstfruits" of those who have died, indicating that His resurrection is the first of many. Paul emphasizes that Christ's resurrection marks the beginning of the end of death, the last enemy to be destroyed.

In describing Christ as the "firstfruits," Paul draws on agricultural imagery to convey the significance of Jesus' resurrection. Just as the first fruits of a harvest signify a greater harvest to come, Christ's resurrection heralds the future resurrection of all believers. This assurance of life beyond death is a cornerstone of Christian hope, offering believers the promise that they, too, will experience resurrection through their faith in Christ. By contrasting the death brought by Adam with the life granted through Christ, Paul underscores the transformative power of the resurrection, which reverses the curse of sin and death and brings new life to humanity.

Furthermore, Paul's assertion that "the last enemy that shall be destroyed is death" encapsulates the essence of the Christian faith. It highlights the ultimate victory of Christ, who reigns until every adversary is vanquished. This reign is not only spiritual but will culminate in a physical manifestation when Christ returns to establish His kingdom fully. The resurrection of Jesus serves as the assurance that death will ultimately be defeated, and in doing so, it empowers believers to live with hope and purpose in the present, knowing that their future is secure in Christ's redemptive work.

Revelation 20:13-14

And the sea gave up the dead which were in it; and death and hell delivered up the dead which were in them: and they were judged every man according to their works. And death and hell were cast into the lake of fire. This is the second death.
Revelation 20:13-14, KJV

The book of Revelation vividly portrays the ultimate defeat of death and Hades. At the final judgment, death and hell will be cast into the lake of fire, symbolizing their complete and eternal destruction. This passage reinforces the theme of Christ's victory over death and the finality of that victory.

This prophetic vision serves as a culmination of the redemptive narrative throughout Scripture, where Christ's victory over sin and death reaches its full realization. The imagery of the sea, death, and Hades delivering up their dead emphasizes the thoroughness of God's judgment, demonstrating that no one can escape accountability for their actions. This judgment highlights the seriousness of life choices and underscores the ultimate authority of God over all realms, including those of death and the afterlife. By bringing every soul before Him for judgment, God affirms His sovereignty and the moral order of the universe, ensuring that justice is ultimately served.

Moreover, the casting of death and hell into the lake of fire signifies the complete eradication of evil and suffering from God's creation. This act represents not just the end of physical death but the obliteration of any power that death and hell once held over humanity. For believers, this promise of victory brings immense hope, affirming that their faith in Christ leads to eternal life and the ultimate restoration of all things. As death is rendered powerless, Christians can live in the assurance that their future is secure in the presence of God, free from fear and pain. This final victory is not merely a theological concept; it is a profound source of comfort and encouragement for the faithful, affirming that in Christ, the end of death is indeed the beginning of everlasting life.

* * *

Again, the early church fathers were instrumental in shaping the theological foundation of Christianity, particularly regarding the interpretation of Scripture related to Christ's victory over death, Hades, and hell. Their writings reflect a deep engagement with the texts and an earnest desire to understand and communicate the implications of

Christ's resurrection for believers. By examining the Old Testament prophecies and New Testament fulfillments, these theologians provided the early church with insights that highlighted the centrality of Christ's triumph over the grave as a pivotal element of the faith. Their teachings served not only to affirm the resurrection but also to inspire believers in their hope for eternal life, grounded in the reality of Christ's victory.

Additionally, the early church fathers contextualized these scriptural passages within the broader narrative of salvation history, connecting Christ's resurrection to the overarching themes of redemption and restoration. They emphasized the transformative power of the resurrection, which not only defeated death but also restored the relationship between God and humanity. This understanding reinforced the belief that, through Christ, believers could confidently approach God, knowing that death no longer held dominion over them. Their interpretations and writings contributed significantly to the church's theological framework, ensuring that the message of victory over death remained a cornerstone of Christian teaching.

For example , Athanasius of Alexandria, in his seminal work *On the Incarnation*, writes:

For since it was necessary also that the debt owing from all should be paid again, for, as I have already said, it was owing that all should die, for which special cause, indeed, He came among us, to this intent after the proofs of His Godhead from His works, to offer also on behalf of all the sacrifice of His body to the Father, as being pure from all spot, and to the end that He might both liberate all from the liability of death, by offering death in place of all, and might also make a new beginning of life for us, by the hope of the resurrection.

On the Incarnation

Athanasius articulates the theological understanding that Christ's death and resurrection were necessary to liberate humanity from the power of death and to inaugurate a new life through the hope of resurrection. In this context, he emphasizes the concept of redemption as a fundamental aspect of the Christian faith. By addressing the "debt owing from all," Athanasius underscores the belief that sin brought about a separation from God, resulting in death's dominion over humanity. This profound need for atonement is met in Christ, who, as the sinless sacrifice, offers Himself to restore the broken relationship between God and humankind. His sacrificial act is not merely a ransom for sin; it is the pivotal moment that redefines the human experience and sets the stage for the promise of eternal life. It is noteworthy at this time to point out that the separation experienced by humanity is not from God's side. God did not become the enemy of man because of their fall and sin; rather, we became enemies from our side. Colossians 1:21 (KJV) states that we became enemies in our own minds. In spite of this, God continues to pursue us.

Moreover, Athanasius draws attention to the transformative power of the resurrection, framing it as the beginning of a new life for believers. Through His resurrection, Christ not only conquers death but also ushers in the hope of resurrection for all who believe in Him. This new beginning signifies a radical shift in the human condition, where death is no longer an endpoint but a passage to eternal life with God. The resurrection serves as the cornerstone of Christian faith, instilling hope and confidence in believers that they, too, will share in this victory over death. Athanasius' insights highlight the integral connection between Christ's resurrection and the overall message of salvation, demonstrating how these theological principles shaped early Christian thought and continue to inspire faith today.

Gregory of Nyssa, also contributed in his work *The Great Catechism*, explains:

He Who delivers man from the calamity of death, and brings him to life again, must of necessity be Himself exempt from death, so that the power of death may not extend further; and thus, by the death of One Who has no part in death, the reign of death should be brought to an end.
The Great Catechism, Chapter 32

Gregory emphasizes that only someone who is not subject to death—Christ—could defeat death. Through His death and resurrection, Christ ends the reign of death, bringing new life to humanity. This assertion highlights the uniqueness of Christ's nature; as both fully God and fully man, He embodies the perfect mediator between humanity and divinity. Gregory's argument underscores the necessity of Christ's sinless life, as only a being without sin could conquer the ultimate consequence of sin, which is death. By becoming a partaker in humanity's suffering and mortality, Christ demonstrates His solidarity with us, yet He remains untouched by the corruption of death.

Furthermore, Gregory's insights reveal the profound theological implications of Christ's victory over death. By voluntarily entering death and then rising from it, Christ dismantles its power and transforms it into a means of liberation. This act not only signifies the defeat of death but also opens the pathway to eternal life for believers. Gregory's teachings encourage a deeper understanding of the resurrection as not merely a historical event but as a transformative reality that enables humanity to experience spiritual renewal and hope. The victory of Christ thus reverberates through the ages, affirming that through Him, believers can triumph over death and embrace the promise of everlasting life.

In one of his famous Easter homilies, John Chrysostom declares:

Hell took a body, and met God. It took earth, and encountered Heaven. It took what it saw, and was overcome by what it did not see. O death, where is thy sting? O grave, where is thy victory? Christ is risen, and you are overthrown. Christ is risen, and the demons are fallen. Christ is risen,

and the angels rejoice. Christ is risen, and life reigns. Christ is risen, and not one dead remains in the grave. For Christ, being risen from the dead, is become the firstfruits of those who have fallen asleep.
Easter Homily

Chrysostom's words encapsulate the triumph of Christ's resurrection. He vividly describes how hell, in taking Christ, encountered God and was defeated. The resurrection of Christ marks the beginning of the end for death and hell, and the beginning of eternal life for believers. Chrysostom's proclamation emphasizes the transformative power of the resurrection, which not only conquers death but also overturns the very foundation of hell. The imagery of hell grappling with God highlights the futility of its attempt to claim dominion over humanity, as it is powerless against the divine authority of Christ.

Moreover, the rhetorical questions "O death, where is thy sting? O grave, where is thy victory?" underscore the profound change that the resurrection brings to the Christian faith. Through Christ's victory, the fear and finality associated with death are rendered void. The resurrection is portrayed not just as an event in history but as a cosmic event with implications for all of creation. As Chrysostom notes, the resurrection heralds a new reality in which life reigns and hope is restored. The rejoicing of angels and the fall of demons signify that Christ's victory is not just for individuals but for the entire spiritual realm. In this context, believers are encouraged to embrace the resurrection as a source of hope and strength, affirming that through Christ, they too will share in the victory over death.

* * *

In the last chapter and this, we have seen a multitude of witness from the biblical writers; both old and the new testaments and also how the early Christians, through a christological reading of the Old Testament, understood the victory of Christ over death, Hades, and hell. This victory is central to a healthy eschatology, offering hope and assurance of the ultimate triumph of life over death, love over fear, and Christ over all the powers of darkness.

Further Reading:

1. Athanasius of Alexandria, *On the Incarnation*, Chapter 20.
2. Gregory of Nyssa, *The Great Catechism*, Chapter 32.
3. John Chrysostom, Easter Homily.

| 4 |

The Scope of Salvation:
Universal or Limited

The question of whether there is hope for those who are in hell has long been a subject of biblical and theological debate for many centuries. This chapter explores whether the redemptive work of Christ extends beyond the Church and beyond death or remains limited. The New Testament provides several passages that suggest a broader application of salvation than merely the present Church. By examining key scriptures, we can better understand the implications of Christ's redemptive work for humanity as a whole.

In Matthew 25:31-46, Jesus describes the final judgment, where the Son of Man separates people as a shepherd separates sheep from goats. This passage emphasizes acts of compassion and justice as criteria for judgment, rather than explicit faith in Christ alone. The "sheep" are commended for their kindness to the "least of these," while the "goats" are condemned for their failure to act compassionately. This portrayal of judgment implies that the scope of salvation may encompass more than just those who explicitly follow Christ. It suggests that those who exhibit compassion and kindness might find favor in the eyes of God, even if they have not had the opportunity to acknowledge Christ directly.

Furthermore, the Gospel of John reinforces this broader understanding of salvation. John 1:9 states, *"That was the true Light which gives light to every man coming into the world."* This statement indicates that Christ's light reaches all people, not just those within the Church. The universal nature of this light challenges the notion of exclusivity in salvation, suggesting that God's revelation through Christ is accessible to everyone, regardless of their background or circumstances. This notion invites us to consider how God's grace and love extend beyond traditional boundaries and expectations.

Moreover, John 1:29 proclaims Jesus as *"the Lamb of God who takes away the sin of the world."* This declaration signifies a comprehensive redemptive purpose that encompasses not only the sins of believers but the entirety of humanity. The phrase "the sin of the world" implies that Christ's sacrificial work is not limited to a select group but rather has implications for all people. This expansive view of redemption prompts a re-evaluation of our understanding of salvation, leading to questions about how it applies to those who have not had the chance to respond to the Gospel in their lifetimes.

The exploration of these New Testament passages reveals a compelling case for a broader understanding of salvation that transcends the limitations of human definitions. While faith in Christ remains essential, the scriptures suggest that God's grace may extend to those outside the conventional boundaries of the Church. As we engage with these theological questions, we are invited to reflect on the depth of God's love and the potential for hope that exists for all of humanity, even beyond the confines of this life. Ultimately, this discourse encourages us to embrace the vastness of God's redemptive plan and to consider the profound implications of Christ's work for those we may presume are beyond hope.

God's Purpose for the World

John 3:16-17 is frequently referenced to highlight the universal nature of God's love and the intention behind Christ's redemptive work. The passage states, *"For God so loved the world that He gave His only begotten Son, that whoever believes in Him should not perish but have everlast-*

ing life. For God did not send His Son into the world to condemn the world, but that the world through Him might be saved." This profound declaration serves to reinforce the notion that the purpose of Christ's coming was to offer salvation to the entire world, not merely to those who immediately accepted Him. This perspective aligns seamlessly with the earlier discussion regarding the broader implications of salvation found in passages like Matthew 25:31-46 and John 1:9. Just as those passages invite us to consider the significance of compassion and the reach of Christ's light, John 3:16-17 emphasizes God's intentional outreach to all humanity. It underscores a divine purpose that transcends exclusivity, illustrating that God's love is not confined to a select group but rather extends to everyone, creating an atmosphere of hope and inclusion.

Moreover, the phrase *"whoever believes"* signifies an openness to faith that is not limited by prior knowledge or experience with Christ. This inclusivity implies that all people, regardless of their past, have the potential to respond to God's love and grace. By stating that God did not send His Son to condemn the world, the text suggests that the primary focus of Christ's mission was redemptive rather than punitive. This emphasis on redemption aligns with the understanding that hope exists even for those who may not have had the opportunity to encounter Christ during their earthly lives. As such, John 3:16-17 complements the earlier scriptural insights by reinforcing the idea that God's plan encompasses a divine love that seeks to redeem all of creation. In this light, we are invited to consider the profound implications of Christ's sacrifice as a beacon of hope for humanity, where every individual, regardless of their circumstances, may find a path to salvation and reconciliation with God. Ultimately, this passage encourages a broader view of God's redemptive purpose—one that is inclusive and full of hope, inviting all people to partake in the eternal life offered through Christ.

The Abundance of Grace

In Romans 5:15-20, the Apostle Paul draws a striking contrast between the consequences of Adam's sin and the overwhelming grace provided through Christ. He begins by stating, *"For if by the one man's offense many died, much more the grace of God and the gift by the grace of the one Man, Jesus Christ, abounded to many"* (Romans 5:15). This powerful assertion highlights that while Adam's disobedience brought death and sin into the world, the grace offered through Jesus is far more abundant and transformative. Paul emphasizes that the effects of sin are significant, yet he quickly follows with the assurance that grace surpasses sin, effectively restoring and elevating humanity beyond its fallen state.

As the passage unfolds, Paul further reinforces this idea with the statement, *"Where sin increased, grace abounded much more"* (Romans 5:20). This declaration suggests that no matter how pervasive sin may be, the grace of God is even more expansive. This notion challenges traditional understandings of salvation, implying that the reach of Christ's grace extends beyond those who explicitly believe in Him. The concept of grace abounding "much more" opens the door to a broader interpretation of salvation, where individuals who may not have had a clear understanding of Christ's redemptive work can still experience God's grace in profound ways.

In the context of hope and inclusion discussed previously, Paul's teaching in Romans complements the earlier passages from Matthew and John by reinforcing the idea that God's grace is available to all humanity, not just to a select few. This aligns with the overarching theme of hope found throughout scripture—God's desire is not for any to perish but for all to come to repentance (2 Peter 3:9). The abundant grace of Christ, therefore, invites us to reconsider the boundaries of salvation and to embrace a vision of divine love that is inclusive, offering hope even to those we might assume are beyond reach.

As we reflect on Paul's powerful words, we are reminded that the abundance of grace provided through Christ not only overcomes the effects of sin but also offers a hopeful pathway for redemption that is accessible to all. This perspective challenges us to recognize the limit-less nature of God's grace and encourages a response of faith and grat-itude, acknowledging that Christ's redemptive work is an invitation for everyone to partake in the gift of eternal life. Ultimately, Romans 5:15-20 serves as a profound reminder of the hope we can share with others, affirming that in Christ, grace truly abounds much more than sin, inviting all to experience the fullness of God's love.

The Ultimate Triumph

Paul's writings in 1 Corinthians 15:24-28 offer a profound vision of Christ's ultimate triumph and the reconciliation of all things. He states, "*Then comes the end, when He delivers the kingdom to God the Father, when He puts an end to all rule and all authority and power*" (1 Corinthians 15:24). This passage highlights the culmination of Christ's mission, where He will ultimately defeat all forms of oppo-sition and establish a reign characterized by divine order and peace. The imagery of Christ delivering the kingdom to God suggests that His redemptive work is not merely about individual salvation but rather encompasses the restoration of all creation. This idea aligns with the broader themes of hope and inclusion previously discussed, emphasizing that God's plan extends beyond the confines of the Church to encompass the entirety of humanity and creation.

Furthermore, Paul's declaration that "*God may be all in all*" (1 Corinthians 15:28) encapsulates the ultimate goal of God's redemptive plan. This vision of universal reconciliation implies that every aspect of creation will be brought into harmony with God's will, culminat-ing in a reality where His presence is fully realized and acknowledged. This prospect challenges traditional views that confine salvation to a select group, instead painting a picture of a God whose love and grace seek to restore all things to Himself. In this light, the concept of God being "all in all" evokes a powerful sense of hope, suggesting that even those who have rejected or remained unaware of Christ will ultimately have an opportunity to encounter the fullness of God's love and grace.

This theme of universal reconciliation resonates deeply with Paul's earlier teachings on the abundance of grace found in Romans 5:15-20. Just as he emphasized that grace abounds where sin increases, the vision presented in 1 Corinthians reinforces the idea that Christ's redemptive work is expansive and far-reaching. It calls us to embrace a hopeful perspective on salvation, recognizing that God's intentions transcend human limitations and assumptions.

In conclusion, Paul's vision of Christ's ultimate triumph in 1 Corinthians offers a compelling narrative of hope and inclusion, suggesting that God's redemptive purpose is comprehensive and unyielding. As we reflect on these passages, we are encouraged to envision a future where all creation experiences the fullness of God's grace and reconciliation. This perspective not only invites us to participate in the work of spreading the Gospel but also compels us to share the hope of universal redemption with others, affirming that God's love has the power to transform and restore all of creation. Ultimately, the promise of Christ's triumph reassures us that, in the end, all will be made new, and God will reign supreme as "all in all."

Universal Acknowledgment

Philippians 2:10-11 reads, "*At the name of Jesus every knee should bow, of those in heaven, and of those on earth, and of those under the earth, and that every tongue should confess that Jesus Christ is Lord, to the glory of God the Father.*" This powerful passage emphasizes a future reality where all beings—whether celestial, terrestrial, or even those in the depths—will recognize and acknowledge Christ's Lordship. The comprehensive nature of this acknowledgment highlights an important aspect of salvation, suggesting that the recognition of Christ's sovereignty is not limited to a specific group but extends universally. This aligns seamlessly with the earlier themes of hope and inclusion, emphasizing that God's redemptive work is aimed at restoring all creation to Himself.

The phrase "every knee should bow" underscores the inevitability of this acknowledgment, portraying a time when all will submit to Christ's authority. This submission is not merely a forced recognition; rather, it is an acknowledgment of His rightful place as Lord over all. The implication here is profound: the scope of salvation is broad enough to encompass every being, indicating that even those who may have lived in opposition to Christ will ultimately come to recognize His sovereignty. This perspective resonates with the previous discussions on universal reconciliation and the abundance of grace, suggesting that God's desire is for all to experience the transformative power of His love.

Moreover, the declaration that "every tongue should confess" further emphasizes the inclusivity of this acknowledgment. It indicates that salvation and recognition of Christ are accessible to all, regardless of their past beliefs or actions. This ties back to the earlier reflections on passages such as John 3:16-17, where the universal nature of God's love is evident. In essence, Philippians 2:10-11 invites us to envision a future where God's grace triumphs over sin and rebellion, culminating in a glorious acknowledgment of Christ as Lord by every individual.

As we contemplate the implications of this universal acknowledgment, we are encouraged to share the message of Christ's Lordship with others. The hope that one day all will bow before Him inspires us to engage in evangelism and ministry with a sense of urgency and purpose. Ultimately, the promise of universal acknowledgment serves as a reminder of the all-encompassing nature of God's redemptive plan, assuring us that in Christ, every person has the potential to experience salvation and reconciliation, leading to a future where God's glory is fully revealed through the acknowledgment of His Son.

Reconciliation of All Things

Colossians 1:20 states that Christ *"reconciles all things to Himself, by Him, whether things on earth or things in heaven, having made peace through the blood of His cross."* This powerful declaration emphasizes the comprehensive nature of Christ's reconciling work, suggesting that it transcends the boundaries of the Church and embraces the entirety of creation. By asserting that all things are reconciled to Himself, the passage indicates that Christ's sacrifice is not limited to a select group of believers but extends to every aspect of the cosmos, promoting a vision of inclusion and hope.

The phrase *"having made peace through the blood of His cross"* highlights the transformative power of Christ's sacrifice. It reinforces the idea that true peace and reconciliation come at a cost—the cost of His life. This sacrificial act is pivotal in understanding the breadth of salvation, as it signifies that Christ's redemptive work addresses not only individual sins but also the larger cosmic disorder introduced by sin. The reconciliation of all things implies a restoration of harmony between God, humanity, and creation, aligning with the earlier themes of universal acknowledgment and ultimate triumph.

Moreover, this concept of reconciliation invites us to reflect on the implications of our role in this divine narrative. If Christ is actively working to reconcile all things, then we, as His followers, are called to participate in this mission. This may involve advocating for justice, promoting peace, and sharing the message of hope found in the Gospel. Embracing our role as ambassadors of reconciliation aligns with the vision presented in *Philippians 2*, where every knee will bow, acknowledging Christ's Lordship and embracing His message of salvation.

Colossians 1:20 provides a powerful affirmation of the universal scope of Christ's reconciling work. By emphasizing that He reconciles all things, this verse reinforces the hopeful narrative that God desires restoration for all creation. As we engage with this truth, we are reminded of our calling to live out the principles of reconciliation in our lives, contributing to the broader mission of bringing all things into alignment with God's will. Ultimately, this passage assures us that God's redemptive plan is comprehensive, offering hope not just for the Church but for the entirety of creation.

God's Desire for All

In 1 Timothy 2:4-6, Paul writes, *"God desires all men to be saved and to come to the knowledge of the truth...who gave Himself a ransom for all, to be testified in due time."* This passage emphasizes that God's desire for salvation is universal, encompassing all people. By stating that God desires "all men to be saved," Paul underscores the inclusive nature of God's redemptive plan, indicating that His grace extends beyond the Church to every individual.

The phrase *"to come to the knowledge of the truth"* further illustrates the purpose behind this universal desire. It suggests that God not only seeks the salvation of humanity but also desires a personal relationship with each person. The truth that God wants all to embrace is rooted in the sacrificial love of Christ, who *"gave Himself a ransom for all."* This act signifies that salvation is available to everyone, reinforcing the idea that God does not wish for anyone to be lost but instead longs for each individual to come to Him.

This universal desire for salvation resonates with the earlier discussion on reconciliation, where the scope of Christ's work extends beyond the confines of the Church. It invites us to reflect on the implications of this truth in our lives and in our outreach to others. If God desires all to be saved, then we, as His followers, are called to share this message of hope and inclusion with those around us, actively participating in the divine mission of reconciliation.

Paul's assertion in this passage highlights the urgency and importance of sharing the Gospel, as it reveals God's heart for humanity. It challenges us to consider how we can embody this desire in our interactions with others, fostering an environment of acceptance and understanding. In doing so, we align ourselves with God's purpose, reflecting His love and grace to a world in need. The message of salvation is not limited to a select few but is intended for everyone, inviting all to respond to God's call and receive His gift of grace.

The Nations and Salvation

Revelation 21:24 describes a vision where *"the nations of those who are saved shall walk in its light."* This imagery suggests that salvation will extend to the nations, reinforcing the idea of a universal scope of salvation. In this context, the term "nations" signifies distinct groups of people, reflecting the diversity of humanity. The vision indicates that, in the culmination of God's redemptive plan, these nations will participate in the eternal life offered through Christ, walking in the light of His presence.

The phrase *"those who are saved"* highlights the inclusive nature of salvation, implying that it encompasses individuals from every nation, tribe, and tongue. This aligns with the earlier themes of reconciliation and God's desire for all to be saved, emphasizing that His redemptive work transcends cultural, ethnic, and geographical boundaries. The imagery of walking in light further symbolizes the transformation and renewal that comes through salvation, as those who have been redeemed now reflect the glory of God.

Additionally, this vision calls attention to the communal aspect of salvation. The idea that nations collectively walk in the light of Christ suggests a future where humanity is united in worship and fellowship. This communal experience of salvation indicates that God's ultimate purpose is not only to save individuals but also to create a harmonious community that reflects His character and love.

In light of this passage, we are encouraged to view salvation as a collective journey that extends beyond our immediate circles. As we engage with others and share the message of hope, we participate in the larger narrative of God's plan for the nations. This perspective inspires us to embrace diversity and inclusivity, recognizing that each nation has a role in the fulfillment of God's redemptive story.

Ultimately, *Revelation 21:24* serves as a powerful reminder of the expansive reach of salvation, affirming that God's grace is available to all people. It challenges us to be vessels of this message, proclaiming the light of Christ to a world in need, and actively participating in the mission of making disciples of all nations.

Healing of the Nations

Revelation 22:2 mentions that *"the tree of life...is for the healing of the nations."* This raises the question: In the new heaven and new earth, why would there be a need for healing, since everyone should be enjoying bliss and living in perfect harmony? Why is healing necessary? I feel that the healing is intended for those outside the city—those judged or supposedly in hell—who will have the opportunity to partake of the tree of life. And no one who takes life will die, because Jesus is the Tree of Life. This powerful imagery supports the concept of universal restoration, indicating that God's redemptive plan encompasses all people even after the final judgement. The tree of life, a symbol of eternal life and divine sustenance, signifies that healing is not limited to physical restoration but extends to spiritual and relational wholeness as well.

The mention of the "healing of the nations" in Revelation 22:2 can be interpreted as symbolic rather than literal, reflecting the ongoing restorative nature of God's love. In the new heaven and new earth, healing could signify the process of reconciliation and renewal for those estranged from God's presence. Some theologians propose that this healing extends even to those outside the New Jerusalem—those judged or separated—indicating that God's grace and the opportunity for restoration remain open. If Christ is understood as the Tree of Life, the healing emphasizes His life-giving essence that transcends death and offers perpetual renewal. This aligns with the idea that no one who partakes of true life in Christ can experience spiritual death, suggesting that the restorative work of God continues beyond judgment. Thus, Revelation's imagery may reflect the hope that no soul is ultimately beyond redemption, as the love of God remains inexorable and boundless.

The phrase "healing of the nations" also suggests a comprehensive renewal, addressing the wounds and divisions that humanity has experienced throughout history. This divine healing points to a future where the brokenness caused by sin, conflict, and suffering will be fully restored. The inclusion of "nations" emphasizes that this healing is for everyone, transcending religious, cultural, and geographical boundaries, reaffirming the universal scope of God's grace and mercy.

Moreover, this imagery resonates with the broader narrative of redemption throughout Scripture. From the beginning, God's desire has been to restore His creation to its intended state of harmony and fellowship. The healing provided by the tree of life symbolizes the culmination of this restorative work, where all people can experience the fullness of life in communion with God and one another.

In light of this passage, we are reminded of our role in participating in God's mission of healing. Just as the tree of life offers sustenance and restoration, we are called to be agents of healing in our communities and among the nations. This involves not only sharing the message of salvation but also actively working towards justice, reconciliation, and compassion in a broken world.

Ultimately, *Revelation 22:2* affirms that God's redemptive plan is expansive, aiming for the healing of all nations. This hope inspires us to engage with others in meaningful ways, reflecting the love and grace of Christ as we anticipate the fulfillment of God's promise for a restored creation.

Early Church Fathers' Perspectives

The early Church Fathers provide valuable insights into the understanding of salvation, reflecting a variety of views on the scope of redemption. Their writings contribute to the ongoing discussion about the universal nature of God's grace and the hope for all humanity.

Origen is known for his belief in apokatastasis, the eventual restoration of all things. He argued that God's ultimate purpose is the reconciliation of all creation, suggesting that, in the end, all souls will be saved and restored to a state of unity with God. Origen's perspective underscores the idea that God's redemptive work is not limited to a select group but is intended for everyone, echoing the biblical themes of universal acknowledgment and healing of the nations.

Similarly, Gregory of Nyssa espoused a form of universalism, believing that God's love would eventually lead all souls to repentance and salvation. His writings emphasize the ultimate goal of God's redemptive plan, envisioning a future where all are reconciled to God. Gregory's insights align with the earlier discussions of salvation's inclusive nature, reinforcing the notion that God's desire extends beyond the Church and reaches every individual.

These early Church Fathers contribute to a broader understanding of salvation that resonates with the scriptural themes of reconciliation, healing, and the hope for all people. Their reflections encourage us to embrace the idea that God's grace is abundant and available to all, prompting us to share this message with those around us.

By considering the perspectives of these early theologians, we gain a richer appreciation for the depth of God's love and the expansive reach of His redemptive plan. Their insights inspire us to actively participate in the mission of healing and reconciliation, reminding us that we are called to reflect God's desire for all to experience His grace and truth. In this way, the legacy of the early Church Fathers continues to inform our understanding of salvation and our role in sharing the hope of Christ with the world.

Modern Theologians' Perspectives

Many modern theologians have contributed significantly to the discussion of salvation and its scope, offering fresh insights that resonate with the themes established by the early Church Fathers. Their perspectives further enrich our understanding of God's redemptive work and its implications for all humanity. I would like to mention three of my favorite theologians in this conversation.

Karl Barth is known for his emphasis on the sovereignty of God and the centrality of Christ in salvation. Barth argued that Christ's redemptive work is comprehensive and all-encompassing. While he did not explicitly advocate for universalism, Barth's theology implies that Christ's work is decisive and ultimately effective for all humanity. This challenges any limitations on the scope of Christ's redemptive work, aligning with the earlier reflections on God's desire for all to be saved and the universal acknowledgment of His sovereignty.

T.F. Torrance developed a robust understanding of atonement and salvation, emphasizing that Christ's reconciliation of humanity with God is both comprehensive and effective. His writings stress the inclusiveness of God's redemptive work while maintaining that a personal response to this grace is essential. Torrance's perspective supports a broad understanding of salvation, resonating with the ideas of healing and restoration found in *Revelation 22:2*. His emphasis on the necessity of individual response complements the themes explored by Origen and Gregory of Nyssa, affirming that while God's grace is abundant, human engagement is also vital.

N.T. Wright has written extensively on the nature of salvation and the kingdom of God, positing that the salvation brought by Jesus is intended to restore all creation. Although he does not explicitly endorse universalism, Wright's writings highlight a broad and inclusive vision of God's redemptive plan. His perspective challenges narrow interpretations of salvation, reinforcing the idea that God's ultimate purpose is the reconciliation of all things, as articulated in *Colossians 1:20*. Wright's emphasis on restoration echoes the sentiments of the early Church Fathers, indicating a continuity of thought regarding the expansive nature of salvation.

Together, these modern theologians contribute to a growing understanding that God's redemptive work is far-reaching and inclusive. Their insights remind us that salvation is not merely an individualistic experience but part of a larger divine narrative that seeks the restoration of all creation. By integrating these contemporary views with those of earlier theologians, we can develop a more holistic perspective on the nature of salvation and the hope it offers to all humanity. This ongoing conversation encourages us to embrace a vision of salvation that is both comprehensive and transformative, inspiring our mission to reflect God's love and grace in the world.

Note: *All scriptures in this chapter are quoted from NKJV except otherwise stated.*

| 5 |

Hell: Various Perspectives

In the discourse surrounding salvation and its scope, the concept of hell often emerges as one of the most contentious and debated topics. Many grapple with questions about the fate of the unevangelized and those unable to make conscious choices, challenging the very foundations of traditional views on eternal punishment. This chapter seeks to address these objections by exploring the multifaceted perspectives on hell, emphasizing the necessity of understanding it through the lens of God's unwavering love and redemptive purpose. By examining scriptural insights, historical interpretations, and contemporary theological reflections, we aim to illuminate how God's justice and mercy extend beyond human limitations, offering a more inclusive understanding of salvation.

Furthermore, the varied interpretations of hell—from infernalism to universalism—invite us to reconsider the traditional notions of divine punishment and explore the transformative potential of God's love. The nature of hell may be better understood not merely as a place of torment but as a condition resulting from humanity's rejection of divine love. In doing so, we will uncover the possibility of post-mortem reconciliation and hope, affirming that God's ultimate desire is the restoration of all creation.

Problem of Unevangelized and Mentally Incapacitated

One valid question is: what will be the fate of those who have not heard the gospel or are incapable of making a conscious choice? Many wonder how a loving and just God can hold individuals accountable for decisions they have not had the opportunity to make. To begin answering that, we must note that the scriptures suggest God's justice and mercy extend beyond human limitations, affirming the belief that divine judgment considers the unique circumstances of each individual. Acts 10:34-35 emphasizes this point, declaring that "God shows no partiality." This implies that God evaluates each person's heart and life context, recognizing that circumstances beyond their control may prevent them from hearing the gospel or fully understanding its implications.

Consider the case of individuals living in remote areas of the world, where access to the gospel is limited or non-existent. They may never encounter the message of Christ due to cultural, geographical, or historical factors. Yet, God's nature as a just and merciful Creator leads many theologians to argue that His judgment will account for these realities. God is not a cruel taskmaster, but a loving Father who desires all to come to Him. This perspective invites a broader understanding of salvation, one that allows for the possibility that God's grace can reach those who have never had the chance to respond to the gospel in this life, highlighting the expansive nature of His redemptive love.

Furthermore, the plight of those who are mentally incapacitated presents another layer of complexity. These individuals may lack the cognitive ability to comprehend or respond to the gospel message, raising questions about their standing before God. Many theologians argue that such individuals are covered by God's grace, as their inability to choose does not negate His love or desire for their salvation. Many have taught that God's justice is intrinsically linked to His mercy and that divine judgment must account for the inherent limitations of human capacity. Ultimately, the broader scope of salvation encompasses not only the unevangelized but also those who, through no fault of their own, cannot make a conscious choice, reinforcing the notion that God's love and mercy transcend human limitations and offer hope for all.

The Nature of Hell and Its Purpose

The issue of salvation and the fate of those who have not heard the gospel or who are incapable of making a conscious choice brings us to the nature and purpose of hell. The modern view of hell as eternal conscious torment is increasingly challenged by the concept of restorative justice. If hell is understood as a place of correction rather than eternal punishment, it aligns with the notion of God's redemptive love. Revelation 22:17 invites those outside to come and take the water of life freely, suggesting a potential for redemption that transcends this life. This perspective not only addresses the fate of the unevangelized but also reflects a broader understanding of God's mercy and the ultimate goal of reconciliation, reinforcing the idea that divine judgment considers the circumstances of individuals (Acts 10:34-35).

The scope of salvation is indeed a complex and multifaceted issue. While modern interpretations often emphasize a limited understanding of salvation, significant scriptural and traditional evidence supports an inclusive and unlimited view. For instance, 1 Timothy 2:4 (ESV) affirms that God "desires all people to be saved and to come to the knowledge of the truth," which underscores the possibility of salvation for all, including those who have not had the opportunity to hear the gospel. Furthermore, the early church fathers explored the idea of universal salvation, suggesting that God's love ultimately prevails over human rebellion. These perspectives challenge prevailing notions of exclusivity and emphasize the transformative power of God's grace, suggesting that even those who seem distant from the message of Christ are encompassed in God's redemptive plan.

By understanding hell through the lens of God's love, we can reconcile the traditional views of eternal punishment with a more hopeful vision of divine justice. This chapter aims to delve deeper into the multifaceted nature of hell, exploring its purpose in light of God's overarching desire for restoration and reconciliation.

Understanding Hell Through the Lens of God's Love

Hell has been a contentious and debated topic throughout Christian history, with varied interpretations and strong opinions shaping its perception. This chapter delves into the multifaceted views of hell, focusing on its nature and purpose, particularly in light of the overarching theme of God's love. By examining the traditional view of hell as eternal conscious torment alongside alternative interpretations, such as restorative justice, we can explore how these perspectives reflect God's character and intentions.

Integrating scriptural insights, historical perspectives, and contemporary theological reflections allows for a comprehensive understanding of hell's role in the divine narrative. For instance, the invitation to partake in the "water of life" signifies God's continual outreach to humanity, emphasizing His desire for redemption. This notion challenges the traditional interpretations of hell and highlights the transformative nature of God's love, suggesting that hell could serve as a corrective rather than merely a punitive experience.

In this context, it becomes crucial to reassess our understanding of hell, recognizing that it may not be contrary to God's nature but instead serves a purpose within His overarching plan for humanity. By viewing hell through the lens of God's love, we can foster a more hopeful and inclusive perspective that aligns with the essential message of the Gospel—that God's desire is for all to come to Him and experience His grace, mercy, and ultimate redemption.

The Varied Perspectives on Hell

The concept of hell is interpreted differently across Christian traditions and theological frameworks. Understanding these perspectives can help us grasp the diversity of thought surrounding hell.

Non-Existence of Hell

The non-existence of hell posits that the concept is a construct of religious institutions designed to instill fear and control over followers. Proponents of this view argue that traditional teachings on hell are not supported by scripture but rather serve to manipulate beliefs and behaviors. This perspective often draws on the idea that a loving God would not condemn any of His creation to eternal suffering, suggesting instead that such beliefs are rooted in human interpretations rather than divine intention.

Advocates for this view may cite passages that emphasize God's love and mercy, such as 1 John 4:8, which states that "God is love." They argue that a loving deity would not subject humanity to endless torment. Instead, they believe that the concept of hell is used to promote adherence to religious doctrines and can lead to spiritual abuse. This interpretation invites a reevaluation of the nature of divine justice and encourages individuals to find meaning and purpose in a life focused on love and compassion rather than fear of punishment.

Psychological State

The psychological state perspective interprets hell not as a physical location but as a metaphor for spiritual desolation and emotional suffering experienced in this life. This view posits that hell represents the internal anguish that arises from separation from God, moral failure, or unresolved guilt. Instead of focusing on eternal punishment, this interpretation encourages believers to confront their psychological struggles and strive for emotional and spiritual healing.

Proponents of this view may draw on scriptures that describe the anguish of the soul, such as Psalm 38:4, where the psalmist expresses deep distress due to sin. They argue that understanding hell as a psychological state can lead to personal transformation and repentance, allowing individuals to experience healing and restoration. This perspective emphasizes the importance of inner work and self-reflection, focusing on the consequences of one's choices and actions rather than the fear of a punitive afterlife.

Infernalism

Infernalism, the traditional view of hell, holds that it is a literal place of eternal conscious torment, often depicted in vivid imagery within Christian literature. This perspective has been prevalent throughout much of modern Christian history, particularly in the medieval period, when descriptions of hell as a fiery pit were used to evoke fear and promote moral behavior. Infernalism underscores the seriousness of sin and the necessity of repentance, positioning hell as a consequence of rejecting God's grace and salvation.

However, this perspective has been increasingly challenged by theologians who suggest that it is inconsistent with the nature of a loving and merciful God. Such critiques advocate for a deeper exploration of God's character and the possibility of redemptive justice, rather than endless punishment. This book leans away from infernalism, aligning instead with views that emphasize God's love, mercy, and restorative purposes in all things.

Annihilationism

Annihilationism asserts that the souls of the damned will ultimately be destroyed or cease to exist rather than enduring eternal punishment. This perspective contrasts sharply with infernalism by suggesting that God's justice is meted out through the ultimate destruction of those who reject Him, rather than endless torment. Annihilationists argue that eternal punishment is incompatible with a loving and just God, proposing instead that the fate of the wicked is final and irreversible.

Supporters of annihilationism may refer to scriptures such as Matthew 10:28, where Jesus indicates that God can destroy both soul and body in hell. They argue that this view upholds the seriousness of sin while also affirming the goodness and love of God, who desires the salvation of all. This perspective invites believers to consider the nature of God's justice and mercy, emphasizing that annihilation is a consequence of rejecting His grace rather than an expression of vindictiveness.

Universalism

Universalism maintains that all souls will eventually be reconciled with God, regardless of their beliefs or actions during their earthly lives. This perspective emphasizes the ultimate restoration of all creation, positing that God's love and grace are so profound that they extend even to those who seem lost. Universalists argue that scriptures affirming God's desire for all to be saved, such as 1 Timothy 2:4, provide a solid theological foundation for this view.

Advocates for universalism may also point to Revelation 21:4, which describes a future where "death shall be no more, neither shall there be mourning, nor crying, nor pain anymore." They contend that this promise extends to all humanity, suggesting that even the most hardened souls will ultimately come to recognize and accept God's love. This perspective challenges traditional views of hell by emphasizing a God who desires reconciliation over punishment, encouraging believers to view salvation as an inclusive and holistic process.

Hell: A Place or a Condition

The concept of hell has been a subject of extensive theological debate, with varying interpretations rooted in biblical texts. The words commonly translated as "hell," such as the Hebrew "Sheol" and the Greek "Hades," primarily refer to the grave or the state of the dead rather than a place of eternal torment. Additionally, the term "Gehenna," originally a physical location outside Jerusalem, evolved into a metaphor for divine judgment. This understanding invites a reevaluation of hell, not merely as a geographical location of punishment but as a complex condition influenced by humanity's relationship with God.

Sheol: In the Old Testament, the term "Sheol" is frequently used to denote the grave or the abode of the dead, devoid of specific implications of torment or punishment. It serves as a neutral term representing the final resting place for all individuals, regardless of their moral standing. For instance, in Psalm 16:10, the psalmist speaks of God not allowing his faithful one to see decay, indicating that Sheol is a state of existence after death, but not necessarily one of suffering. Thus, Sheol encompasses a broader understanding of mortality and the inevitability of death, transcending moral distinctions. Furthermore, the absence of punishment associated with Sheol suggests a more inclusive perspective on the afterlife. It reflects the belief that all people, both the righteous and the wicked, share the same fate in death, awaiting eventual resurrection or judgment. This notion challenges the traditional view of hell as solely a place of torment, emphasizing that Sheol embodies a shared human experience. As such, it prompts believers to consider the nature of death and the hope for redemption beyond this life.

Hades: Similarly, the New Testament employs the term "Hades" to describe the realm of the dead, often mirroring the connotations of Sheol. Hades is depicted not necessarily as a place of punishment but as a temporary holding area for souls. For example, in Luke 16:23, the rich man finds himself in Hades, experiencing torment, yet this narrative emphasizes his prior choices in life rather than establishing Hades as a permanent state of suffering. This view highlights the possibility of Hades serving as a transitional state, awaiting the final resurrection and judgment. Moreover, the understanding of Hades as a temporary condition reinforces the idea that existence after death is not fixed but contingent on one's relationship with God. The biblical narrative suggests that while Hades may entail separation from the divine, it does not imply an irrevocable state of torment. This interpretation encourages a more nuanced understanding of the afterlife, wherein Hades becomes a space for reflection and accountability rather than an eternal prison. Consequently, this perspective invites believers to consider the implications of their earthly lives and choices in shaping their ultimate destiny.

Gehenna: In the New Testament, "Gehenna" emerges as a term that Jesus uses to depict a place of future judgment, symbolizing the grave consequences of moral and spiritual failure. Originally, Gehenna referred to a valley outside Jerusalem where refuse was burned, evoking images of destruction and desolation. Jesus' reference to Gehenna underscores the seriousness of sin and the resulting separation from God, as seen in Matthew 5:22, where He warns that those who insult others are in danger of judgment. This metaphor serves to illustrate the dire consequences of rejecting divine love and moral responsibility. Moreover, the use of Gehenna as a metaphor for judgment reinforces the idea that hell is not merely a physical location but a condition reflecting one's choices and relationship with God. It signifies a state of existence marked by spiritual separation and the absence of God's presence, which can be experienced as torment or anguish. This perspective invites believers to engage in self-reflection and repentance, acknowledging that the consequences of their actions can lead to profound spiritual disconnection. In this way, Gehenna serves as a poignant reminder of the gravity of sin and the importance of embracing God's love and grace.

* * *

Therefore, hell may be understood as both a place and a condition, though not necessarily a physical location. It represents a state of being where individuals experience separation from God due to their rejection of divine love and presence. This separation can manifest in various ways, depending on one's relationship with God. For some, this may be experienced as a profound sense of emptiness or despair, while for others, it may reflect the consequences of unrepentant sin.

Ultimately, this understanding invites a deeper exploration of the nature of hell, emphasizing that it is not merely a place of punishment, but a condition rooted in the choices made in life and the resulting distance from the divine.

Common Misconceptions About Hell

A prevalent misconception is that hell is a place where God is absent. Some interpret hell as a location where God's presence is entirely removed, suggesting a form of divine abandonment that leaves souls in a state of despair without any hope. This view often arises from a misunderstanding of the nature of God's omnipresence. In contrast, Paul's letter to the Colossians challenges this interpretation by stating, "*For by him all things were created... all things have been created through him and for him*" (Colossians 1:16 WEB). This passage affirms that God is present and sustaining all things, which implies that no part of creation, including hell, is truly outside of God's presence.

Moreover, the depiction of hell in Scripture supports the idea that God's presence is integral to the experience of the damned. For instance, Revelation 14:9-10 describes the torment of the damned occurring "*in the presence of the holy angels and in the presence of the Lamb.*" This imagery indicates that even in hell, God's presence is felt, albeit in a manner that may evoke anguish rather than comfort for those who have chosen to reject Him. Such interpretations underscore the complexity of God's relationship with creation, where His presence can bring about different experiences based on individuals' responses to Him.

The early church father Origen of Alexandria elaborated on this understanding of divine presence by arguing that God's omnipresence extends to all realms, including hell. He famously stated, "*God is in all things, and nothing can be outside of Him*". This perspective aligns with the view that God's presence is not absent from hell but rather transforms the nature of the experience based on one's response to Him. Therefore, rather than being a place devoid of God's influence, hell can be understood as a state where the consequences of one's choices are fully realized in the context of God's constant and sustaining presence.

The Redemptive Nature of Hell

Reinterpreting the traditional image of hellfire in the New Testament requires a significant shift in perspective—from viewing it as a manifestation of divine anger to recognizing it as an extension of God's purifying love. The New Testament frequently employs fire imagery when discussing judgment and consequences, yet these depictions can be understood not merely as punitive measures but rather as expressions of God's transformative purpose. The consistent message throughout scripture is that God embodies boundless love and compassion, suggesting that even the harshest realities, such as the fires of hell, may serve a restorative function. When we reframe hellfire in this light, we begin to understand it as a crucial component of God's overarching plan to reconcile and redeem His creation, ultimately reflecting His unwavering desire for wholeness in every aspect of existence.

A compelling example of this compassionate divine nature is found in Matthew 5:44 (NKJV), where Jesus instructs believers to "love your enemies." This call to love is not merely a suggestion but rather an imperative that mirrors the very nature of God—who is characterized by patience and mercy. Furthermore, 1 Corinthians 13:5 (NKJV) highlights that divine love is neither "provoked" nor does it seek harm, further reinforcing the idea that God's actions are rooted in compassion. If God is portrayed as one who does not count people's sins against them, as stated in 2 Corinthians 5:19 (NKJV), then it follows that our understanding of hellfire should evolve from one of punitive retribution to a view that embraces restoration and reconciliation. Instead of envisioning hell as a realm of endless suffering meted out by an angry deity, we can begin to see it as a manifestation of God's intense, persistent love, which aims to draw all individuals back into a relationship with Him.

In this recontextualization, hellfire becomes a symbol of purification rather than punishment. The fires of hell can be interpreted as a powerful force designed to cleanse and refine the soul, stripping away all that hinders a person's relationship with God. This aligns with the broader theological view that God desires to restore humanity, even those who have strayed far from His embrace. The idea that God's fire is meant for purification underscores the belief that every aspect of divine judgment ultimately reflects His commitment to love and redemption. This perspective shifts the narrative from one of fear and condemnation to one of hope and transformative potential, suggesting that even the most challenging experiences are ultimately part of God's loving plan.

Hebrews 12:29 (NKJV) states, "Our God is a consuming fire," which encapsulates the essence of divine love and its purifying nature. This fire is not meant to destroy but to refine, highlighting the profound intensity of God's love that seeks to engage even those who resist it. For individuals unwilling to embrace this divine love, the experience of hellfire may feel like anguish or suffering, illustrating the stark contrast between accepting and rejecting God's grace. In this way, the fire of God's love serves as a means of purification, demonstrating that His desire for wholeness extends to all, even to those who find themselves in opposition to Him. This interpretation challenges believers to reassess their understanding of hell, moving away from fear-based notions towards a perspective that emphasizes God's longing for connection and restoration.

The theological insights of Karl Barth further illuminate this understanding of hellfire as an expression of God's purifying love. Barth emphasized that God's love is the most powerful force in the universe and possesses the ability to burn away everything that is not aligned with it. In his view, the fire of hell is not an act of divine retribution; rather, it reflects God's desire for transformation and healing. Barth's assertion invites us to reconsider hell not as an end but as a means through which God actively pursues the restoration of all creation. This understanding encourages believers to embrace a theology of hope, one that recognizes that God's love is unrelenting and seeks to reclaim even those who seem lost.

Ultimately, the reframing of hellfire as a tool for purification and restoration offers a transformative perspective on the nature of divine judgment. By understanding hell not as a place of eternal torment but as a reflection of God's deep love and desire for reconciliation, believers can find hope in the promise that God's grace is greater than human rebellion. This understanding invites a more profound exploration of God's character, emphasizing that His love transcends all barriers and seeks to bring every soul back into harmony with Him. By embracing this perspective, believers can live in the assurance that even in the face of the most challenging circumstances, God's ultimate aim is restoration, not retribution, reaffirming the profound truth that divine love will always prevail.

Torment and Love

The concept of torment in hell can be understood as the reaction of those who reject God's love rather than as an active infliction of suffering by God. This perspective highlights the inherent tension between divine love and human rejection, illustrating how the experience of hell may stem from an unwillingness to accept the grace and mercy offered by God. When individuals choose to turn away from this love, the natural consequence is a state of separation that can be experienced as torment. Rather than portraying God as a punitive figure, this understanding of hell emphasizes the tragic reality of human choices and their repercussions.

Romans 12:20-21 describes loving one's enemies as akin to *"heaping fiery coals on their head,"* suggesting that acts of kindness can lead to discomfort or realization in those who oppose it. This imagery serves to reinforce the idea that love has a profound impact, capable of provoking introspection and, ultimately, a response. In a similar vein, the fire of God's love may burn away resistance and rebellion in those who have chosen to reject Him. The discomfort experienced by those who resist this love is not a product of divine malice but rather a reflection of the stark reality of separation from the source of all good and life. It is a sobering reminder that rejecting love inevitably leads to suffering, which serves to highlight the beauty and necessity of divine grace.

Exodus 24:16-18 depicts the glory of the Lord on Mount Sinai as *"a consuming fire."* This fire, though terrifying to some, represents divine holiness and love. The same divine fire can be experienced differently depending on one's response to it. For those who seek God and embrace His love, this fire may illuminate their path and cleanse their hearts. In contrast, for those who reject His presence, the consuming fire serves as a reminder of what they have chosen to forfeit—a relationship marked by love and acceptance.

Let us look at another passage:

10 "Now I will arise," says the Lord,
"now I will lift myself up;
now I will be exalted.
11 You conceive chaff; you give birth to stubble;
your breath is a fire that will consume you.
12 And the peoples will be as if burned to lime,
like thorns cut down, that are burned in the fire."
13 Hear, you who are far off, what I have done;
and you who are near, acknowledge my might.
14 The sinners in Zion are afraid;
trembling has seized the godless:
"Who among us can dwell with the consuming fire?
Who among us can dwell with everlasting burnings?"
15 He who walks righteously and speaks uprightly,
who despises the gain of oppressions,
who shakes his hands, lest they hold a bribe,
who stops his ears from hearing of bloodshed
and shuts his eyes from looking on evil,

16 he will dwell on the heights;
his place of defense will be the fortresses of rocks;
his bread will be given him;
his water will be sure.
Isaiah 33:10-16 ESV

Isaiah 33:10-16 presents a vision of divine judgment, where some experience it as a consuming fire while others find it a place of refuge. This passage illustrates how the same divine presence can be perceived differently based on one's moral and spiritual condition. Those attuned to God's love find shelter in His presence, while those who resist it encounter the discomfort of their estrangement.

N.T. Wright argues that the concept of hell should be seen in the context of God's redemptive purposes. According to him, hell is not the result of God's vindictive anger but a manifestation of God's just love, which can be experienced as torment by those who reject it. Wright's view emphasizes that hell reflects the consequences of rejecting divine love rather than an arbitrary punishment. This understanding encourages a reexamination of hell as a complex interplay between divine justice and mercy, inviting individuals to consider the implications of their choices in relation to God's profound desire for reconciliation. The nature of torment in hell, therefore, serves as a poignant reminder of the transformative power of love, both divine and human, and the tragic cost of its rejection.

The Possibility of Post-Mortem Reconciliation

The question of whether there is any chance for reconciliation for those in hell remains a contentious topic within theological discussions. On one side, infernalists maintain that there is no hope of salvation after death, asserting that hell is a final and irreversible state for those who reject God. This view emphasizes the seriousness of moral choices made during one's earthly life and highlights the concept of divine justice. Conversely, universalists argue for the eventual reconciliation of all souls, believing that God's love and mercy will ultimately prevail, extending beyond death to bring restoration to every individual.

One of the early proponents of universal reconciliation was Origen of Alexandria, who suggested that all souls would eventually be restored to God. In his seminal work *De Principiis*, he posits that *"The end of all things is the restoration of the whole creation to its original state of unity and harmony."* Origen's vision presents a hopeful outlook that transcends the limitations of earthly existence, emphasizing God's intention to restore creation and reconcile every soul to Himself. This perspective suggests that God's love is so profound that even the most hardened hearts may one day be softened and drawn back into the fold of divine grace.

Karl Barth also highlighted the hope of universal restoration, emphasizing the mystery of divine grace. He presented in his monumental work Church Dogmatic that the final goal of history is the reconciliation of all things in Christ, which includes the hope of salvation for all humanity. Barth's assertion reinforces the notion that God's purpose in Christ encompasses all of creation, advocating for a future where reconciliation is achieved. He challenges believers to hold onto the hope that, despite the current state of the world, God's ultimate plan is one of love and restoration, rather than despair and separation.

Furthermore, N.T. Wright addresses this theme in his writings, explaining that the ultimate aim of God's redemptive plan is the restoration and reconciliation of all things in Christ, suggesting that the final chapter is not one of eternal separation but of universal restoration. Wright's perspective encourages believers to envision a future where God's love triumphs over all forms of division and brokenness. He challenges traditional notions of hell as an unending separation from God, proposing instead that God's redemptive work is continually at play, even in the lives of those who have departed from this world.

As we navigate these complex theological waters, it is important to acknowledge that the final resolution regarding post-mortem reconciliation remains uncertain. Scriptures offer a diverse array of perspectives on this issue, with passages that suggest both judgment and hope. For instance, *Romans 11:32 (ESV)* states, *"For God has consigned all to disobedience, that he may have mercy on all."* This verse underscores the idea that God's mercy extends to all, even those who may initially reject Him. As we await further understanding, we are called to cultivate hope in Christ, who embodies our ultimate hope and reconciliation.

* * *

Hell, while a profound and challenging topic, must be understood through the lens of God's love. The nature of hell—whether as a place or a condition—reflects our response to divine love rather than merely serving as a punitive measure. It is a manifestation of the choices we make concerning our relationship with God, emphasizing the importance of free will in our spiritual journeys. Our understanding of hell should align with the overarching theme of God's love, which is inclusive, redemptive, and ultimately victorious.

In the coming chapters, we will explore the biblical and historical perspectives on post-mortem reconciliation and hope, continuing our journey into the depths of eschatological truth. By examining various theological viewpoints, eastern orthodoxy and scriptural references, we aim to shed light on the possibility of reconciliation beyond death and reaffirm the message of hope embedded in God's redemptive plan. Through this exploration, we can better appreciate the complexities of divine love and the invitation extended to all humanity for reconciliation and restoration.

Further Reading

1. Barth, Karl. *Church Dogmatics.*
2. Lewis, C.S. (1952). *Mere Christianity.* New York: Macmillan.
3. McGrath, A.E. (2011). *Christian Theology: An Introduction.* Wiley-Blackwell.

4. Origen of Alexandria. *De Principiis.*

5. Stott, J. (1988). *The Cross of Christ.* Downers Grove, IL: Inter-Varsity Press.

6. Wright, N.T. *Surprised by Hope.*

| 6 |

Eastern Orthodox Views

The Eastern Orthodox Church offers a profoundly Christ-centered vision of the afterlife, where the focus is not on punishment or retribution but on the transformative love of God. In Orthodox theology, the presence of God is inescapable and all-encompassing, meaning that every soul will stand before Him, embraced by His eternal love. However, the experience of this presence will vary from person to person, depending on the state of their soul and its openness to divine love. For some, God's love will be a source of unimaginable joy, while for others it may be experienced as discomfort or anguish—not because God punishes, but because of the inner disposition of the individual soul.

This perspective invites a reconsideration of common notions about heaven and hell. Unlike the rigid dichotomy of eternal reward and retribution found in some traditions, Orthodox theology understands hell not as a physical location or divine-inflicted punishment but as a *state of being*. It is the experience of God's love through the lens of a heart unprepared to receive it. In this framework, the "fire" often associated with hell is not external torment but the fiery love of God experienced differently by those who resist or reject it. The Orthodox Church emphasizes that the afterlife is not a legalistic judgment but a revelation of truth—the truth of who God is and who we are in relationship to Him.

Redemption in the Orthodox tradition is deeply connected to *theosis*—the process of becoming one with God, transformed into His likeness through union with Christ. This journey does not end with death but continues into eternity. Salvation, therefore, is not a static event but an ongoing process in which humanity is invited to participate. The afterlife is the fulfillment of this journey: the culmination of God's redemptive work in Christ, where every person is confronted with His divine presence and invited into deeper communion with Him.

This chapter delves into how redemption, theosis, and the afterlife interweave in the Orthodox understanding of humanity's ultimate destiny. It also explores the Church's distinctive interpretation of hell as a relational reality—one that reflects God's unchanging love, rather than divine wrath or retribution. Through this lens, the afterlife is revealed not as a system of rewards and punishments but as a continual encounter with the living Christ. This encounter, personal and communal, highlights that in Christ, all things are made new, even beyond the boundaries of time, death, and human expectation.

Thus, the Orthodox view of the afterlife invites us to embrace the mystery of God's love and the hope that all creation will be restored in Him. Heaven and hell are not separate realms governed by divine decree but different experiences of the same divine reality. In the end, God's unrelenting love is what awaits every soul—not to condemn, but to transform and draw all things into the fullness of life in Christ.

Hell as the Experience of God's Unmediated Love

In Orthodox theology, hell is not defined by the absence of God but by the experience of His unmediated presence. This presence, though universally given, is perceived differently depending on the individual's inner disposition. Those who embrace God's love experience it as radiant joy and life-giving communion, while those who reject it encounter the same love as discomfort, sorrow, or torment. Hell, in this sense, is not an externally imposed punishment but an internal state—a reflection of the human heart that has chosen to turn away from divine love.

St. Isaac the Syrian offers a profound insight into this paradox: *"It is wrong to think that sinners in hell are deprived of the love of God... But love acts in two different ways: it torments sinners... but it gives delight to those who have observed its duties."* This teaching illustrates a central principle of Orthodox theology—God is love, and His love never changes. What changes is the heart that encounters Him. The torment of hell arises from the inability or refusal to accept and participate in the love that God offers freely to all. The unrepentant heart, hardened and self-centered, experiences the same divine love that brings joy to the righteous as a burning, purifying fire. This fire is not the expression of God's anger but of His love, which relentlessly seeks to cleanse and restore.

The Apostle Paul captures this dynamic in 1 Corinthians 3:13: *"...the fire will test the quality of each person's work."* This fire, symbolic of God's presence, reveals the true nature of each person's life, motivations, and actions. For those whose lives are built on love, faith, and humility, the fire is a refining agent that reveals their communion with God. For those whose lives are built on pride, selfishness, and rejection of grace, the fire is experienced as painful exposure. Yet, even this pain carries within it the potential for redemption—a call to transformation through the unyielding presence of divine love.

The Orthodox understanding of hell challenges the notion of a dualistic afterlife divided into separate realms of reward and punishment. Rather than depicting hell as eternal separation from God, it emphasizes the universality of God's presence. Hell is the experience of divine love resisted and misunderstood. It is a relational reality—a tragic yet profound consequence of free will, where the human soul, created for communion with God, suffers from its own refusal to embrace that communion.

This perspective reveals the seriousness of human freedom and the weight of our choices in shaping our eternal destiny. Yet, it also highlights the hope that even the soul in torment is not beyond the reach of God's love. The fire of hell is not a fire of destruction but one of purification—a fire that continues to offer the possibility of repentance, renewal, and healing. As Orthodox theologians often emphasize, God's love never ceases; it is inexorable, persistent, and ever-inviting.

Thus, hell is not a final condemnation but an invitation—even in the midst of pain—to return to the source of life and love. The love of God, though it may burn the unprepared heart, is always oriented toward restoration and renewal. Every soul, even in its most stubborn resistance, remains the object of God's desire for reconciliation. In this light, the Orthodox vision of the afterlife is not centered on fear but on the hope that love will ultimately prevail. Hell, then, is not God's rejection of humanity but humanity's ongoing struggle to accept the God who never stops loving.

The Role of Human Freedom and Self-Imposed Separation from God

In Orthodox theology, human freedom is regarded as a sacred gift from God, fundamental to the nature of love and relationship. This understanding emphasizes that hell is not a punishment imposed by a vengeful deity, but rather the natural outcome of choices made by individuals. Just as the journey toward *theosis*—the process of becoming united with God—requires the active and willing cooperation of the human will with divine grace, hell represents the tragic consequence of the soul's refusal to participate in this divine life.

As we have seen previously, St. Athanasius encapsulates this profound truth with his assertion: *"God became man so that man might become god."* This quote reflects the essence of the Christian call to transformation through Christ, inviting humanity into a deeper relationship with the divine. While God extends an offer of redemption and transformation to all, the reality remains that some individuals may choose to reject this invitation. The refusal to accept God's grace and love leads to a state of self-imposed separation, which is the true essence of hell.

This concept of self-imposed separation highlights a crucial aspect of Orthodox thought: the intrinsic connection between freedom and love. Love cannot be coerced; it must be freely given and freely received. God respects the human will, even when that will leads to choices that result in separation from Him. Hell, therefore, becomes a manifestation of the profound respect God has for human freedom, even when it is misused.

The implications of this understanding are profound. In the Orthodox view, hell is not a place of eternal torment designed for retribution but rather a state of existence that reflects the internal disposition of the soul. When individuals choose to reject the divine invitation to love, they inevitably isolate themselves from the source of all life and goodness. This separation can lead to a painful awareness of what is lost—the joy of communion with God and the fulfillment that comes from participating in His love.

Moreover, this self-imposed separation is not static; it is a dynamic state characterized by ongoing choices. Each decision to turn away from God further distances the soul from the source of life, deepening the experience of hell. In this light, hell becomes an existential reality rooted in the conscious rejection of divine love and grace. It is a condition marked by an absence of fulfillment, peace, and joy—the fruits of life lived in harmony with God.

Yet, the Orthodox tradition also holds that God's love remains ever-present, even in the depths of separation. While hell is experienced as a consequence of the human choice to turn away, it does not signify God's abandonment of humanity. His love persists, seeking to draw the estranged soul back to Himself, continually inviting it to return. This ongoing invitation reflects the profound mystery of God's grace, which respects human freedom while simultaneously longing for reconciliation.

The interplay of human freedom and divine love encapsulates the essence of the Christian life. Each individual is called to discern the path they will take—whether toward communion with God and the joys of *theosis* or into the isolating shadows of separation. This call to freedom is both a privilege and a responsibility, urging believers to recognize the weight of their choices and their ultimate implications for their eternal destiny.

Thus, in Orthodox thought, hell serves as a poignant reminder of the sanctity of human freedom and the transformative power of love. It challenges us to reflect on our relationship with God and the profound choices that shape our lives. While God extends His hand in grace and love, the ultimate decision lies with each individual, for it is in our freedom that we truly encounter the depth of divine love and the reality of our existence in relation to Him.

Redemption, Theosis, and Participation in Divine Life

The concept of *theosis*, or deification, stands as a cornerstone of Eastern Orthodox theology. This transformative process signifies the profound reality of human beings being shaped into the likeness of God through active participation in His divine life. In the Orthodox view, salvation is not merely about evading hell or securing a place in heaven; it is fundamentally about achieving true union with God. This intimate communion begins in the present life and extends into the afterlife, inviting believers into a dynamic relationship with the divine.

Participation in *theosis* involves a multifaceted approach to spiritual growth that encompasses prayer, the sacraments, and a life committed to virtue. Through regular engagement in these practices, individuals begin to experience the transformative power of God's grace in their lives. Prayer serves as a vital conduit for this connection, facilitating an ongoing dialogue with God that nurtures the soul and opens the heart to divine love. The sacraments, as visible manifestations of grace, are seen as essential means through which believers partake in the life of Christ, deepening their connection to Him and to one another. Living virtuously—embodying the teachings of

Christ in daily life—also plays a crucial role in this journey, as it aligns the believer's will with God's and cultivates the fruits of the Spirit.

This understanding of salvation through *theosis* sharply contrasts with many Western interpretations, which often frame salvation as a legal transaction—where sin is accounted for, and salvation is granted in a courtroom-like scenario. In Orthodox theology, however, salvation is understood as a holistic process of healing and restoration, addressing the wounds of sin and the brokenness of the human condition. This perspective invites believers to view the question of hell not merely as a matter of divine judgment but as a poignant consideration of missed opportunities for transformation and growth in God's love.

As St. Gregory of Nazianzus eloquently states: *"We shall become gods to the extent that we participate in God."* This quote encapsulates the essence of *theosis*—the idea that our capacity to become more like God is directly related to our willingness to engage in the divine life. The more we open ourselves to God's grace and actively participate in His life, the more we reflect His image and character. Conversely, the tragic result of refusing this offer of transformation is hell—a state of existence marked by disconnection from divine love, a failure to grow, and a life devoid of true fulfillment.

For Orthodox Christians, redemption is not a static event confined to a singular moment but an ongoing journey toward deeper unity with God. This journey invites believers to continually seek God's presence, allowing His grace to work within them, transforming their hearts and minds. It is an ever-unfolding process of becoming, where the faithful are called to strive for holiness and participate actively in the life of the Church, which serves as the Body of Christ on earth.

In this context, hell is not merely a place of punishment but a poignant reminder of what is lost when one chooses to turn away from the transformative offer of divine love. It represents a failure to fulfill the potential for growth and communion with God. The Orthodox understanding emphasizes that redemption is accessible to all; it is a gift freely offered to every person, yet it must be actively received and engaged with through the exercise of human freedom.

Thus, the journey toward *theosis* becomes a pathway not only to personal transformation but also to communal renewal. As individuals grow in their union with God, they contribute to the life of the Church and the world, reflecting the love and grace they have received. This collective journey reinforces the interconnectedness of all believers in the pursuit of holiness, reminding us that our participation in divine life has implications that extend beyond ourselves.

Ultimately, the Orthodox vision of redemption through *theosis* invites us to embrace our potential as beloved children of God, to seek transformation in His love, and to recognize that our choices have the power to shape our eternal destiny. As we embark on this sacred journey, we are continually reminded of the beauty and depth of the life we are called to participate in—a life that leads us ever closer to the heart of God.

Apocatastasis: Hope for Universal Restoration

A distinctive and compelling aspect of Eastern Orthodox thought is the concept of *apocatastasis*, which embodies the profound hope that all souls will ultimately be reconciled to God. This belief offers a vision of salvation that transcends the boundaries of human understanding, suggesting that divine love possesses an irresistible quality capable of drawing even the most wayward souls back to their Creator. The early Church Father St. Gregory of Nyssa articulated this hope with eloquence, firmly believing that God's love, in its essence, is victorious over all forms of rejection and alienation. He famously expressed this conviction by stating: *"Evil will cease to exist, for nothing that is contrary to nature can endure forever."*

This assertion underscores the belief that evil, in its various manifestations, is fundamentally at odds with the inherent goodness and order established by God. It implies that any separation from the divine—a state often characterized as hell—cannot last indefinitely, as it is not aligned with the ultimate purpose of creation. In this view, hell is envisioned not as an eternal prison, but rather as a temporary state of existence that may eventually be transformed by the overwhelming power of divine love.

While the concept of *apocatastasis* is not formally codified as a dogma within the Orthodox Church, it nevertheless reflects a hopeful and inclusive vision of God's mercy and grace. This theological perspective resonates deeply within the heart of Orthodoxy, emphasizing the boundless compassion of God who desires the salvation of all people. The idea encourages believers to embrace a more optimistic outlook on the afterlife, fostering a sense of hope that transcends despair.

St. Gregory's insights challenge the notion of a finality in damnation, proposing instead that the divine plan encompasses the eventual reconciliation of all souls, regardless of their earthly choices. This notion invites contemplation on the nature of repentance, suggesting that even those who have strayed far from God's embrace may ultimately encounter the transformative power of His love. The belief in *apocatastasis* inspires a profound trust in the mystery of God's redemptive work, reminding believers that the scope of God's mercy extends beyond human limitations.

However, it is important to note that the Orthodox Church approaches this topic with a sense of humility and reverence, acknowledging the mystery surrounding God's judgment. While the hope for universal restoration offers a vision of optimism, the Church refrains from presuming to dictate the specifics of how God will enact this final reconciliation. The complexity of God's nature and the intricacies of divine justice are recognized, inviting believers to remain open to the profound mysteries of faith.

The belief in *apocatastasis* also invites a deeper understanding of the relationship between human freedom and divine love. It suggests that while individuals possess the freedom to reject God, this freedom does not negate the possibility of eventual acceptance and transformation. In the end, the divine desire for reconciliation may inspire a change of heart, leading even the most estranged souls back to the embrace of God. This hope challenges believers to view others—especially those who seem lost or beyond redemption—with compassion and understanding, recognizing that the journey toward restoration may take unexpected paths.

Furthermore, the concept of *apocatastasis* nurtures a vision of community rooted in love and grace. It invites believers to actively participate in the work of reconciliation in their own lives, fostering relationships that reflect the inclusive nature of God's love. By embodying mercy, compassion, and forgiveness, the faithful contribute to the unfolding of God's plan for restoration, aligning their lives with the divine purpose.

Ultimately, the vision of *apocatastasis* serves as a powerful reminder of the expansive nature of God's love and the hope that undergirds the Christian faith. It invites believers to hold onto the promise that, in the end, all will be made right, and every soul will have the opportunity to be reconciled with their Creator. This hope not only shapes the way Christians approach the afterlife but also profoundly influences their engagement with the world around them, fostering a spirit of love, compassion, and unity that reflects the heart of the Gospel.

The Last Judgment and the Revelation of True Relationship

In Orthodox eschatology, the concept of the Last Judgment transcends the simplistic notion of condemnation; it is fundamentally about the revelation of each individual's relationship with God. On that momentous day, every person will stand before the divine presence, encountering the profound truth of who they are in relation to their Creator. This revelation will be marked not by punitive measures but by an unveiling of the genuine state of the heart and soul—a reflection of one's choices and relationship with divine love throughout their earthly existence.

The experience of the Last Judgment is characterized by a duality: the righteous will find immense joy and fulfillment in God's presence, basking in the warmth of His love and grace. They will experience a deep sense of communion with God, where their lives of faith and virtue are fully realized in the eternal embrace of divine love. This joy is rooted in the understanding that their choices aligned with God's will, allowing them to partake in the divine life in a meaningful way.

Conversely, those who have consciously rejected God will experience a different reality. For them, the presence of God will be felt as torment, not due to an arbitrary act of punishment, but as a natural consequence of their self-imposed separation from divine love. The fire of God's love, which brings joy to the righteous, will be perceived as a consuming force for those who have turned away, illuminating the choices they made and the relationships they neglected. This experience echoes the sentiment expressed by Orthodox theologians who emphasize that hell is not merely a place, but a state of being—an ongoing reality shaped by one's relationship with God.

Orthodox liturgy profoundly reflects this understanding through its frequent prayers for the departed. These prayers are not merely ritualistic but reveal a deeply held belief in the transformative power of prayer and its capacity to effect change, even beyond death. By entrusting the departed to God's mercy, the faithful affirm the hope that through divine grace, even those who have passed away may experience healing and restoration. This liturgical practice underscores the communal aspect of faith, where the living intercede for the souls of the departed, expressing love, compassion, and solidarity in the journey toward redemption.

The prayers for the dead serve as a powerful reminder that, in Orthodox thought, the relationship between God and humanity is never severed, even by death. The Church believes that God's love knows no bounds and that His desire for reconciliation extends even to those who have strayed far from Him. This hope infuses the liturgy with a sense of expectation, as the faithful gather to pray not only for those who have passed but also for their own spiritual journeys, recognizing that every soul is valued and loved by God.

Moreover, the Last Judgment is seen as an opportunity for every individual to fully understand their relationship with God in its entirety. This encounter serves to clarify the essence of God's love and justice, revealing that divine judgment is fundamentally rooted in love. Rather than a moment of fear or trepidation, the Last Judgment becomes a moment of profound truth—an unveiling of the heart's true intentions and a recognition of how each life reflects or distorts the image of God.

As Orthodox Christians approach the reality of the Last Judgment, they are called to cultivate a relationship with God characterized by love, repentance, and humility. This preparation involves an ongoing commitment to live in accordance with the teachings of Christ, fostering virtues such as compassion, forgiveness, and mercy. By doing so, believers align themselves with the transformative power of God's love, ensuring that their ultimate encounter with Him is one of joy rather than torment.

In this context, the Last Judgment emerges as a hopeful and redemptive moment in the journey of the soul. It invites believers to reflect on their lives, encouraging them to engage deeply with their faith and to seek a relationship with God that is authentic and life-giving. Ultimately, it is a reminder that every person is invited into a deeper communion with God, where love prevails, healing occurs, and the promise of eternal life is fulfilled.

Liturgical Expressions of the Afterlife: Prayers for the Departed

Orthodox worship is rich in liturgical expressions that honor and remember the deceased, with prayers for the dead woven throughout various services and rituals. These prayers express profound hope in the mercy and forgiveness of God, reflecting the belief that life continues after death and that God's love transcends the boundaries of mortality. The acknowledgment that God's grace reaches into the realm of the dead is a cornerstone of Orthodox theology, emphasizing that no soul is beyond the redemptive reach of divine love.

One of the central expressions of this belief is the *Memorial Service*, known as the *Panikhida*. This service is a solemn yet hopeful gathering where the community comes together to pray for the departed. It serves as a powerful reminder that the connection between the living and the dead is not severed by death; rather, it highlights the ongoing relationship that exists within the body of Christ. During the Panikhida, the faithful offer prayers, light candles, and share memories of those who have passed, fostering a spirit of love and remembrance.

The service typically includes readings from Scripture, hymns, and prayers that express a deep yearning for the departed souls to experience God's mercy. The prayers often invoke the names of the deceased, calling them into the community's consciousness and affirming their place within the Church. Through these liturgical acts, Orthodox Christians convey their love for those who have departed and their hope for their eventual reconciliation with God.

All Souls' Days are another significant liturgical observance within the Orthodox Church, dedicated to praying for the departed. These days, which occur several times throughout the liturgical calendar, provide opportunities for the faithful to come together specifically to remember and intercede for their loved ones who have passed away. The collective nature of these observances underscores the communal aspect of faith, where the Church on earth stands in solidarity with the Church in heaven.

During these services, the congregation prays for the forgiveness of sins, the peace of the departed souls, and their entrance into eternal life. The prayers articulate a profound theological belief: that the grace of God is not limited to the earthly realm but permeates all existence, reaching those who have left this life. This underscores the Orthodox conviction that God's love is all-encompassing and eternal, capable of touching every soul, regardless of their earthly circumstances.

While the Orthodox Church does not formally teach *apocatasta-sis*—the hope for universal restoration—as dogma, the spirit of this belief is nevertheless present in the liturgical prayers. The prayers for the departed reflect a deep-seated hope that God's mercy can touch all souls, fostering a sense of optimism and assurance. The faithful are invited to participate in the healing process of the departed, believing that their prayers can assist in the souls' journey toward divine grace and reconciliation.

Moreover, the prayers for the dead serve as a reminder of the interconnectedness of all believers within the Body of Christ. This understanding fosters a sense of unity that transcends time and space, as the Church on earth remains in communion with the Church in heaven. This mystical connection reinforces the belief that love endures beyond death and that every soul is valuable in the eyes of God.

In these liturgical expressions, the Orthodox tradition acknowledges the reality of death while simultaneously affirming the hope of resurrection and eternal life. The prayers for the departed are not merely rituals of remembrance; they are acts of love and faith that echo the ultimate victory of Christ over death. As the faithful engage in these practices, they are reminded of the profound truth that God's love is a force that seeks to heal and restore, reaching even into the depths of the afterlife.

Ultimately, the liturgical expressions of the afterlife, exemplified through prayers for the departed, reinforce the Orthodox understanding of salvation as a journey towards divine communion. They remind the faithful that, in the face of death, hope remains alive through God's unfathomable mercy, inviting all souls into a loving relationship with Him.

The Mystery of Hell and the Afterlife: Balancing Hope and Freedom

The Orthodox Church presents a nuanced understanding of the afterlife, where the concepts of hope and human freedom coexist in a delicate balance. While the Church holds out the hope of salvation for all, it also acknowledges the profound mystery of human freedom, which is intrinsic to the nature of love. In this theological framework, hell is not viewed as a predetermined divine decree but rather as a manifestation of love that is ultimately rejected. This perspective invites a deeper exploration of the relationship between divine love, human agency, and the consequences of our choices.

Orthodox theology emphasizes that God's love is unchanging and ever-present. The Church Fathers teach that while God desires all of humanity to be saved and come to the knowledge of the truth (1 Timothy 2:4), the experience of that love varies based on the state of each soul. The Apostle Paul poignantly articulates this in Romans 2:4, noting that it is God's kindness that leads to repentance. However, this kindness can also evoke a contrasting response in those who choose to turn away, highlighting the tension between divine grace and human rejection.

This balance between hope and freedom is critical to the Orthodox understanding of hell and the afterlife. It recognizes that God's invitation to communion is always extended, but the choice to accept or reject that invitation lies with the individual. Each person must respond to God's love freely, reflecting the intrinsic nature of love itself, which cannot be compelled or forced. The Church respects this freedom, understanding that true love allows for the possibility of rejection.

Furthermore, this perspective fosters a sense of hope, rooted in the belief that God's mercy and love are vast enough to embrace all souls. The idea that no one is beyond redemption resonates deeply within Orthodox thought. Even the most wayward soul retains the potential for repentance and reconciliation, reflecting the unwavering nature of God's grace. In this sense, hell is not an end but a consequence of the choices made in life, an existential state of separation from the fullness of God's love.

The mystery of hell serves as a profound reminder that the choices made in this life have eternal significance. While the Church teaches that God's love is available to all, it also affirms that the refusal to accept that love leads to a reality that feels like hell. The experience of hell, then, is not merely about punishment; it is an existential experience of disconnection from the source of life and love.

In this framework, the Orthodox tradition does not shy away from the complexities of human freedom. Instead, it embraces them, acknowledging the weight of individual choices while holding onto the hope that God's love can ultimately reach even the farthest corners of the human heart. This duality is essential to Orthodox eschatology, inviting believers to live in a way that aligns with God's will while recognizing the seriousness of the choices that shape their eternal destinies.

Ultimately, the mystery of hell and the afterlife in Orthodox theology invites believers into a profound engagement with the concepts of hope, love, and freedom. It acknowledges the reality of human choice while affirming that God's desire is for every soul to find its fulfillment in Him. In this way, the Orthodox understanding of the afterlife is not merely a reflection on judgment but an invitation to explore the depths of divine love and the transformative power of grace. It encourages the faithful to respond to God's love actively and to live out their faith in a manner that reflects the hope of salvation, knowing that the journey towards God is marked by both freedom and divine invitation.

The Eastern Orthodox concept of the afterlife presents a profound and multifaceted understanding of the relationship between God and humanity. Central to this vision is the unwavering belief that God's love is both inexorable and ever-present, permeating every aspect of existence. In this framework, hell is not seen as a punishment arbitrarily inflicted by God; rather, it is understood as the natural consequence of rejecting His love. This perspective redefines the experience of hell, positioning it not as a place of retribution but as a state of being that reflects the soul's own choices and its relationship with the divine.

In Orthodox theology, redemption transcends the simplistic notion of merely avoiding hell. It invites individuals into a transformative journey of participation in divine life, culminating in the process known as theosis. This concept emphasizes that salvation is not just a legal transaction but a healing and restoration of humanity's original purpose—union with God. The journey toward theosis is marked by a deepening relationship with the Creator, where believers are called to cooperate with divine grace and strive for a life reflective of God's love and righteousness.

The notion of universal salvation, or apocatastasis, embodies a hopeful vision within the Eastern Orthodox tradition. While not a dogmatic teaching, it reflects the belief that God's love ultimately has the power to reconcile all souls to Himself. This hope underscores the conviction that even those who find themselves in hell may, through the infinite mercy of God, eventually experience repentance and restoration. The idea that evil will ultimately cease to exist reinforces the notion that God's love is relentless, pursuing every soul with the intent of drawing them back into communion with Him.

Ultimately, the Orthodox Church teaches that the afterlife is not a final destination but a continuation of the soul's journey toward God. Both the joy of heaven and the torment of hell are experiences of the same divine presence, felt differently based on the soul's response to God's love. For the righteous, God's presence brings joy, fulfillment, and peace, while for those who have rejected Him, that same presence is experienced as torment. This duality serves as a reminder of the importance of one's choices in life and the eternal implications of those choices.

In conclusion, the Eastern Orthodox understanding of hell, redemption, and the hope of theosis invites believers to embrace a vision of the afterlife that is rich in mystery and grace. It challenges the faithful to reflect on their relationship with God and encourages them to live in a manner that actively participates in the divine life. By recognizing that God's love is ever-present and transformative, individuals are empowered to seek union with Him, experiencing the fullness of life that comes from accepting His love. In this journey, hope remains central—a hope grounded in the belief that God's desire is for all to be saved, offering the promise of reconciliation and the ultimate fulfillment of humanity's destiny in Christ.

Further Reading

1. St. Isaac the Syrian: *Ascetical Homilies*
2. St. Athanasius the Great: *On the Incarnation*
3. Ware, Timothy: *The Orthodox Way* (Orthodox Christian Publications Center, 1993)
4. Lossky, Vladimir: *The Mystical Theology of the Eastern Church* (St. Vladimir's Seminary Press, 1976)
5. St. Gregory of Nyssa: *On the Human Condition*
6. St. Gregory of Nazianzus: *Theological Orations*
7. Hodgson, P. C.: *Salvation: A History* (Wm. B. Eerdmans Publishing Co., 2009)

| 7 |

Is There Hope for Those Who Are in Hell?

In the ongoing exploration of eschatological themes, we confront one of the most challenging questions: *Is there hope for those who find themselves in hell?* This inquiry has long divided theologians and scholars, sparking intense debates that touch upon the very essence of divine justice and mercy. On one side, infernalists assert an unequivocal "No," arguing that hell represents a final and irreversible state of punishment for the unrepentant. They maintain that the existence of hell underscores the seriousness of sin and the ultimate accountability of individuals before a holy God. Conversely, universalists offer a resounding "Yes," suggesting that God's love and grace extend even into the darkest corners of existence. They posit that divine redemption is available to all, proposing a transformative hope that transcends the boundaries of human understanding.

Navigating these divergent views requires a comprehensive examination of Scripture, where various passages present contrasting images of judgment and salvation. Engaging in earnest prayer allows us to seek divine wisdom, reflecting on the nature of God, who is Love itself. This chapter aims to explore the theological implications of both positions while considering the overarching narrative of redemption that runs throughout the biblical text. As we journey through this complex landscape, we will also contemplate the philosophical and ethical dimensions surrounding the concept of hell, aiming to arrive at a nuanced understanding that respects the depth of God's character and the mysteries of divine justice. Ultimately, this exploration is not just an academic exercise; it is a deeply personal quest for answers to some of life's most profound questions.

Infernalism vs. Universalism

Infernalism, the belief in eternal conscious torment, asserts that those condemned to hell endure unending punishment without hope of redemption. Advocates of this view often cite scriptures like Matthew 25:46, which mentions "eternal punishment," and Revelation 20:10, describing the devil being tormented "day and night forever." Infernalists argue these verses emphasize the severity of sin and the unyielding nature of divine justice, warning that rejecting God's grace results in permanent separation from Him. For them, hell reflects the glory of God's righteousness by displaying His final triumph over evil and ensuring moral accountability.

However, this interpretation of key texts is increasingly challenged. The phrase "eternal punishment" in Matthew 25:46, for example, is derived from the Greek word *aionios*, which can mean "pertaining to an age" rather than endless time. Likewise, Revelation 20:10, written in symbolic apocalyptic language, is better understood as expressing the ultimate defeat of evil rather than literal, infinite suffering. Many theologians argue that these passages, when viewed in context, do not support the notion of eternal torment but instead reveal God's justice as restorative, not retributive.

In contrast, universalism teaches that all will ultimately be saved, grounded in the belief that God's love and grace will triumph over judgment. Universalists highlight scriptures like 1 Timothy 2:4, which declares that God "desires all people to be saved and to come to the knowledge of the truth," and Romans 5:18, where Paul affirms that "just as one trespass brought condemnation for all, so one righteous act resulted in justification and life for all." They argue that God's mercy is not limited by human rejection and that Christ's redemptive work will reconcile all people to God in the end. This hopeful vision of salvation emphasizes that God's justice serves His love, ultimately restoring even those who once lived in rebellion.

Both infernalism and universalism draw upon biblical texts to support their claims, but the interpretation of these texts often reveals significant theological differences. For instance, infernalists might point to verses that emphasize the finality of judgment, while universalists focus on scriptures that highlight God's unconditional love and the hope for redemption. However, proof-texting—using isolated scriptures to support a predetermined view—can obscure the broader biblical narrative and the multifaceted nature of God's love and justice. When verses are taken out of context, they can be wielded as weapons in theological debates, leading to divisive and oversimplified conclusions about complex doctrines.

This contentious debate raises important questions about the character of God. Does divine justice necessitate eternal punishment, or is God's mercy so profound that it can overcome even the gravest of sins? The implications of these views extend beyond theology into ethics, pastoral care, and personal faith. Those who embrace infernalism believe that the reality of hell serves as a powerful motivator for evangelism and moral living. They often use the fear of eternal separation from God to compel individuals to respond to altar calls and to share that sense of urgency with others. However, this fear-based approach often leads to spiritual anxiety and fosters a distorted understanding of God's nature, portraying Him as solely punitive.

On the other hand, universalism offers a message of hope and inclusivity, emphasizing that no one is beyond the reach of God's love. This perspective can foster a sense of unity and compassion among believers, encouraging them to embrace a broader view of salvation. Yet, some critics argue that universalism risks diminishing the seriousness of sin and the necessity of repentance, potentially leading to a lax attitude toward moral behavior and spiritual accountability.

Ultimately, the debate between infernalism and universalism challenges us to grapple with the depth and breadth of God's nature. It compels us to consider how we interpret Scripture and how our beliefs about hell impact our understanding of divine justice and love. As we delve deeper into this complex discussion, we must strive to honor the mystery of God's character while remaining faithful to the truths revealed in the biblical narrative. The journey through this theological landscape requires humility, open-mindedness, and a commitment to seeking a holistic understanding of God's plan for humanity, one that encompasses both justice and mercy, judgment and grace. In doing so, we may discover a richer and more profound appreciation for the nature of salvation and the eternal destiny of all people.

Scriptural Evidence of Hope for All

The Bible contains numerous passages that hint at a more inclusive and far-reaching salvation, inviting readers to reconsider the limits of God's redemptive plan. While certain scriptures appear to emphasize judgment, others highlight the depth of God's mercy and His ultimate desire for reconciliation. This tension invites careful reflection, as it suggests that divine justice and mercy are not opposing forces but work in harmony to accomplish God's purpose for creation. Rather than focusing exclusively on eternal condemnation, many texts point toward restoration, healing, and the eventual triumph of grace. Such an interpretation challenges narrow views of salvation, urging believers to adopt a more hopeful vision of God's plan for humanity. While we have examined some of these verses in previous chapters, it is beneficial to explore them again to reinforce the point until it fully sinks in.

When the Son of Man comes in His glory, and all the angels with Him, He will sit on His glorious throne. All the nations will be gathered before Him, and He will separate the people one from another as a shepherd separates

the sheep from the goats. He will put the sheep on His right and the goats on
His left.
Matthew 25:31-33, NIV

This passage presents a compelling account of the final judgment, where individuals are separated based on their acts of mercy and kindness. The emphasis on tangible actions of love—feeding the hungry, welcoming strangers, and visiting the sick—highlights a broader scope of divine justice and mercy. Rather than focusing solely on faith or doctrinal adherence, this text suggests that God's evaluation of humanity includes the demonstration of compassion and care for others. This raises the possibility that even those who may not explicitly identify with Christ or the Church may still be embraced by God's redemptive plan through their acts of love.

What is particularly striking in this passage is the inclusivity of the judgment. All nations are gathered before Christ's throne, suggesting that God's justice transcends religious boundaries and national affiliations. The sheep, those commended for their compassionate acts, are not identified by their theological knowledge or religious status but by their willingness to care for "the least of these." This implies that divine mercy reaches beyond conventional religious frameworks, acknowledging the presence of God's love at work in people's lives, even when it is not explicitly labeled as such. It offers a vision of salvation that is rooted in the character of God—who is love—and challenges believers to reflect that same love in their interactions with the world.

Behold, the Lamb of God, who takes away the sin of the world!
John 1:29, ESV

This verse reinforces the perspective of an expansive salvation when John the Baptist identifies Jesus. The use of the term "world" (*kosmos*) hints at a salvific work that extends beyond just the Church or a specific group of believers. It speaks to the universal reach of Christ's mission, affirming that His sacrificial death carries redemptive implications for all of humanity, not merely for those who consciously follow Him. This understanding challenges the notion of a limited atonement, suggesting instead that the scope of salvation is as vast as creation itself, embracing every person and offering hope even to those outside traditional religious frameworks.

Moreover, the imagery of the Lamb evokes the concept of substitutionary sacrifice, but here it is applied universally—Christ bears the sin of the entire world, not just a select few. This invites readers to consider the depth of God's grace, which flows freely to all, regardless of their response or religious identity. The focus is on what Christ *has accomplished* rather than what individuals must do to earn or secure salvation. It underscores the sufficiency of His redemptive work, challenging believers to trust in the far-reaching power of God's mercy to reconcile all things to Himself in due time. This verse encourages a vision of salvation that is cosmic in scope, reflecting the heart of a God who desires to restore and renew all of creation.

Again in the popular verse John 3:16-17, we read: *"For God so loved the world that he gave his only Son, that whoever believes in him should not perish but have eternal life. For God did not send his Son into the world to condemn the world, but in order that the world might be saved through him."* (John 3:16-17, ESV). Here, the emphasis is on the universality of God's love and the redemptive purpose behind Christ's coming. The language suggests that salvation is intended for the entire world, underscoring the idea that God's desire is not for anyone to be lost. This passage serves as a cornerstone for the universalist perspective, emphasizing that Christ's mission was fundamentally about saving humanity rather than condemning it.

John 12:32 states: *"And I, when I am lifted up from the earth, will draw all people to myself."* (John 12:32, ESV). This declaration points to a universal drawing towards Christ, indicating that His crucifixion serves as a pivotal moment of attraction for all individuals. The implication here is significant; it suggests that Christ's sacrifice has the power to reach beyond cultural, religious, and temporal boundaries. This notion of a universal draw invites a broader understanding of who can respond to God's grace and mercy, reinforcing the idea that hope exists for all people, including those who may have never had the opportunity to hear the Gospel in their lifetime.

Together, these scriptures imply that Christ's redemptive work encompasses more than just the current Church age, reinforcing the notion that hope exists for those who may have otherwise been deemed lost. The exploration of these texts encourages a dialogue that transcends simplistic categorizations of salvation, urging us to consider the complexities of divine love and justice. As we reflect on these passages, we must grapple with the implications of a God whose desire is to redeem, restore, and reconcile all of creation to Himself. In doing so, we open ourselves to a more expansive view of salvation that acknowledges both the seriousness of sin and the depths of God's grace. This broader understanding fosters a sense of hope and encourages believers to approach the topic of salvation with humility, compassion, and a commitment to sharing the transformative love of Christ with all.

Pauline Perspectives on Hope for All

The Apostle Paul provides further insight into the scope of salvation, articulating themes that suggest the possibility of redemption for all. His writings reflect a profound grasp of God's grace, emphasizing that salvation is not limited by human failure but is rooted in the faithfulness of Christ. Paul consistently underscores the universal impact of Christ's sacrifice, presenting it as a remedy not only for individual sins but for the brokenness of the entire world. Through his teachings, he highlights God's relentless desire to reconcile all creation to Himself, suggesting that divine mercy extends beyond temporal boundaries to offer hope even to those who resist or reject grace in this life. Paul's vision of salvation portrays Christ's redemptive work as transformative, not merely transactional—an act that brings healing, restoration, and new life for all people.

Let us now carefully examine a couple of key verses to explore how they contribute to this broader understanding of salvation. *Therefore, as one trespass led to condemnation for all men, so one act of righteousness leads to justification and life for all men. For as by one man's disobedience the many were made sinners, so by one man's obedience the many will be made righteous.* Romans 5:18-19, ESV. This passage highlights the parallel between Adam's disobedience and Christ's righteousness. Paul indicates that just as Adam's sin brought condemnation to all humanity, Christ's act of righteousness has the potential to bring justification and life to all. This reinforces the concept that the righteousness of Christ can rectify the disobedience of Adam, extending the possibility of salvation to every individual. The implication here is profound: if the consequences of one man's actions can affect all, so too can the redemptive work of Christ. This understanding fosters hope that no one is beyond the reach of God's grace.

In 2 Corinthians 5:19, Paul writes: *God was in Christ reconciling the world to Himself, not counting their trespasses against them.* (2 Corinthians 5:19, ESV). In this verse, reconciliation is described as a universal act, emphasizing God's intent to restore humanity. Paul's use of the term "the world" suggests an expansive scope of God's redemptive work, which transcends cultural, ethnic, and religious barriers. This assertion underscores that God's desire is not limited to a specific group but encompasses all of creation, inviting everyone into a relationship with Him. By stating that God is not counting their trespasses against them, Paul emphasizes the overwhelming grace that characterizes God's approach to humanity. This perspective invites believers to adopt a posture of grace and reconciliation towards others, reflecting the heart of God in their interactions.

1 Timothy 2:4 further illustrates this universal desire: *God desires all people to be saved and to come to the knowledge of the truth."* (1 Timothy 2:4, ESV). Paul expresses a clear and unequivocal desire for the salvation of every soul. The phrase "all people" emphasizes that God's intention is inclusive, inviting everyone to partake in His saving grace. This universal aspiration for salvation underscores the hope that ex-

ists for every individual, regardless of their past or present circumstances. Paul's message here aligns with the overarching theme of God's love, which is not restricted by human limitations but seeks to embrace all.

Additionally, in Ephesians 1:9-10, Paul writes: *"Making known to us the mystery of His will, according to His purpose, which He set forth in Christ as a plan for the fullness of time, to unite all things in Him, things in heaven and things on earth."* (Ephesians 1:9-10, ESV) This passage reveals God's overarching plan to unify all creation in Christ. The phrase "all things" indicates a comprehensive scope, suggesting that God's redemptive work will ultimately encompass everything. This perspective reinforces the notion that salvation is not merely a transaction for the few who believe but a cosmic restoration that God desires for all of creation.

Finally, Philippians 2:9-11 asserts: *"Therefore God has highly exalted Him and bestowed on Him the name that is above every name, so that at the name of Jesus every knee should bow, in heaven and on earth and under the earth, and every tongue confess that Jesus Christ is Lord, to the glory of God the Father."* (Philippians 2:9-11, ESV). This passage points to a future where all of creation acknowledges the lordship of Christ. The imagery of "every knee" bowing and "every tongue" confessing suggests a universal recognition of Christ's authority, emphasizing that God's redemptive plan ultimately leads to a restoration of right relationship between Him and humanity.

These passages underscore that God's redemptive work through Christ is not confined to the Church but extends to all humanity, inviting us to reflect on the nature of divine love and mercy. Through Paul's writings, we are reminded that God's grace is boundless and that His desire for reconciliation encompasses every individual. This encourages believers to embrace a hopeful perspective on salvation, recognizing that it is not merely for the few but a gift available to all who are willing to receive it.

The Problem of Exclusivism

Adopting an exclusivist or infernalist view presents significant theological and ethical challenges that require careful examination. These challenges not only raise questions about the nature of God but also compel us to reflect on the implications of our beliefs regarding salvation and judgment.

Children and the Mentally Incapacitated: A pressing concern within the exclusivist framework is the fate of children who die before reaching an age of accountability or individuals who are mentally incapacitated. The strict exclusionary view must address these vulnerable groups and the implications for a loving God who desires that all come to salvation. Are these individuals condemned to eternal punishment due to circumstances beyond their control? Such a notion seems incompatible with the character of a just and merciful God. The question arises: Does God's love extend to those unable to comprehend the message of salvation? The challenge here is to reconcile the idea of divine justice with the reality of innocent lives, raising the possibility that God's grace may encompass those who cannot respond to the Gospel.

The Unevangelized: Another significant challenge arises when considering the millions of people who have lived and died without ever hearing the Gospel. This reality poses a critical question: Does the lack of opportunity for salvation imply eternal exclusion for these individuals? If so, how does that align with the belief in a loving and just God? The exclusivist view struggles to account for those who never had the chance to know Christ, raising concerns about the fairness of divine judgment. Can we trust in God's justice and mercy to find a way for those who did not know Him? This dilemma invites a more nuanced understanding of God's salvific plan, one that may extend beyond human comprehension and traditional boundaries.

Morally Upright but Unbelieving Individuals: Additionally, we must consider the fate of marlly upright individuals who, despite their kindness and moral integrity, never embraced Christianity. This scenario poses a profound theological conundrum: Can we reconcile the eternal punishment of morally upright people with a loving and just God? The existence of individuals who exemplify virtue but do not adhere to a particular faith tradition challenges the notion that faith alone determines one's eternal destiny. If God is indeed a loving and just judge, how can the exclusion of such individuals be justified? These questions challenge the traditional view of a punitive hell without hope, suggesting that a strict infernalist perspective does not account for the complexities of human experience or the depth of God's mercy and justice.

The ethical implications of exclusivism extend beyond individual cases; they compel us to examine the broader narrative of God's love as revealed in Scripture. The notion that a loving God would condemn countless individuals to eternal torment for circumstances beyond their control or lack of exposure to the Gospel seems increasingly untenable. Instead, we are invited to explore the possibility that God's grace is more expansive than we can fully understand, and that His desire for reconciliation and redemption is at the heart of His nature.

Furthermore, these challenges encourage a reevaluation of how we engage with others in our spiritual journeys. If we genuinely believe in a God of love, how does that shape our interactions with those who differ in belief or have not had the opportunity to know Him? The exclusivist perspective may inadvertently foster an environment of fear and condemnation, while a more inclusive view invites compassion, understanding, and a commitment to share the message of hope with all humanity.

In summary, the problems presented by an exclusivist view compel us to grapple with difficult questions about God's justice and mercy. The challenges posed by the fate of children, the unevangelized, and righteous but unbelieving individuals underscore the need for a theological framework that recognizes the complexity of divine love. As we navigate these issues, we must remain open to the possibility that God's redemptive work extends far beyond our limited understanding, inviting us into a deeper appreciation of His character as a loving and just Creator.

Hope and Restoration

I propose that there is hope for all because God's love is infinite, His mercies endure forever, and His wrath and anger are for a moment. In fact, James 2:13 (NKJV) states that "mercy triumphs over judgment." This highlights the profound truth that while God is just, His mercy ultimately prevails. God has reconciled all men to Himself, but some who have not perceived that reality are living in a state of perishing. When they die in that state, they may experience hell; however, I maintain that God's judgment is not retributive but restorative. I advocate for "Hope for all" as the safest and most biblical position regarding the spiritual salvation of the human race. The scope of the sacrifice of Jesus Christ will ultimately extend beyond the 'little flock' of the Church in this world to embrace a greater majority. The Word of God provides strong hints that this will occur, even though we often overlook many illuminating Scriptures due to the influence of Christian writers and theologians who have focused primarily on the Church in the present world without considering what lies beyond that.

Consider the Jesus who particularly sought out the outcasts of His day—publicans, sinners, and Samaritans. Is it not likely that He would also seek after other lost individuals? Such perseverance is evident in the parables of the lost coin, the lost sheep, and the Prodigal Son, which all demonstrate a God who actively seeks the lost. With such a will to seek after the lost, can we credibly suggest that He would create billions of people while intending for a significant majority to end up in eternal hell for the 'rejection' of a God whom many never even knew? We must also ask whether such a fate can be reconciled with a God who forgave those who hated Him, persecuted Him, and tortured Him before cruelly executing Him (Luke 23:34). I maintain that those who do not entertain this hope possess a view that is sadly and seriously distorted, even though it is often proposed by very sincere people. Such a perspective is perilously close to the fatalism of the pagans and the dualism that seems to have emerged from figures like Plutarch, suggesting that good and evil will always coexist because neither God nor Satan can challenge each other's domains. If we posit that, at the end of time, hell has a vast 'population'—a belief held by many modern Christians—can that truly reflect the biblical assertion that every knee will ultimately bow to Christ?

Revelation 22:15-17 states:

15 For without are dogs, and sorcerers, and whoremongers, and murderers, and idolaters, and whosoever loveth and maketh a lie.
16 I Jesus have sent mine angel to testify unto you these things in the churches. I am the root and the offspring of David, and the bright and morning star.
17 And the Spirit and the bride say, Come. And let him that heareth say, Come. And let him that is athirst come. And whosoever will, let him take the water of life freely. (KJV)

In this passage, God's Spirit and the Bride (the saved Church, represented by the New Jerusalem) issue an invitation to those who were once outside—those who are suffering in hell, referred to as "dogs," "sorcerers," etc.—to come and drink of the water of life. The earlier chapters of Revelation (20-21) reveal that the tree of life is for the healing of the nations—the judged nations that were destined for hell. These images show that God is actively at work to restore, offering hope to those who find themselves outside of His grace.

It is crucial to clarify that my position of hope is not universalism. Universalism asserts that all will finally be saved; I contend that while some may reject the unrelenting and inexorable love of God, I doubt that many will do so. However, Scripture leaves us no room to dogmatize our hope for the salvation of all. I am fully aware of the awe-inspiring power and righteous judgment (restorative justice) of God, and His holy judgment cannot be compromised!

I assert that those who do not allow room for hope overlook too many Scriptures that clearly look beyond God's dealings with the Church in the present world and at this present time. Without a doubt, there will be broadness in God's mercy. After all, God will display His grace in the age to come, as affirmed in Ephesians 2:7 (ESV): *"So that in the coming ages he might show the immeasurable riches of his grace in kindness toward us in Christ Jesus."*

While hell remains a place of torment—fiery coals that should be avoided—the only way out of hell, both in this age and the age to come, is through Jesus Christ. We need to preach this Gospel: that Jesus is the best thing that has happened to the world. As people awaken to the consciousness of Christ within them, they can experience the hope and joy of bliss that springs forth from this age into the ages of ages (everlasting).

* * *

In conclusion, my stance on hope emphasizes that God's redemptive love is expansive and inclusive. It challenges us to consider the implications of His mercy and justice, presenting a vision of a God who deeply desires reconciliation and restoration. While we recognize the reality of hell as a consequence of rejecting God's grace, we also affirm that His ultimate aim is to bring all people to Himself through His love and mercy. This perspective compels us to live and share the Gospel in a manner that reflects the boundless nature of God's love, extending an invitation to all, and cultivating a hopeful outlook for the future.

Further Readings

1. The Universal Christ: How a Forgotten Reality Can Change Everything We See, Hope For, and Believe by Richard Rohr

2. Love Wins: A Book About Heaven, Hell, and the Fate of Every Person Who Ever Lived by Rob Bell
3. All Shall Be Well: An Approach to the Theology of Julian of Norwich by John T. McNeill
4. The Great Divorce by C.S. Lewis
5. Surprised by Hope: Rethinking Heaven, the Resurrection, and the Mission of the Church by N.T. Wright

| 8 |

Hope Beyond Hell

In the previous chapter, we examined the profound question of whether there is hope for those in hell, highlighting the diverse theological perspectives that frame this contentious debate. While infernalism presents a bleak view of eternal damnation, and universalism offers an optimistic outlook on the potential for salvation, the nuances of this discussion require a more comprehensive exploration. This chapter continued to delve deeper into the scriptural foundations and theological implications surrounding the hope for those in hell. By analyzing key biblical texts, we can discern that a hopeful perspective rooted in God's character—defined fundamentally by love—may indeed offer a more compelling understanding of divine justice and mercy. This theological exploration invites us to reflect on the broader implications of Christ's redemptive work and God's impartiality, encouraging us to consider the expansive scope of salvation that may extend even beyond our traditional confines of understanding. It is also very crucial to understand that proof-texting—using isolated biblical verses to support a particular doctrine—is not a reliable method for comprehensive biblical interpretation. Such an approach often leads to a truncated view of the complex and multifaceted nature of Scripture. Instead, we should consider the broader essence of God's character, which is fundamentally defined by love. This divine love compels us to explore the depths of God's mercy, grace, and the implications of Christ's redemptive work as we seek to understand this profound question.

One foundational text that we examined in previous chapter is John 1:29 (ESV), which states, "Behold the Lamb of God, who takes away the sin of the world!" This verse underscores the comprehensive nature of Christ's atonement. According to Augustine of Hippo, this statement reflects the universal scope of Christ's sacrificial death, intended to cover the sins of all humanity, not just a select group. Augustine asserts that Christ's work was not limited by human divisions but was a deliberate act of grace aimed at all people

Further reinforcing this idea, John 3:16-17 (NKJV) proclaims, "For God so loved the world that He gave His only begotten Son, that whoever believes in Him should not perish but have everlasting life. For God did not send His Son into the world to condemn the world, but that the world through Him might be saved." The universal language in these verses is significant. The Reformed theologian John Calvin acknowledged this as indicative of God's intent to provide salvation to all humanity, not merely the believers, emphasizing that God's salvific purpose extends to the entire world, underscoring His boundless love.

Another important verse we looked at is John 12:32 (NKJV): "And I, if I am lifted up from the earth, will draw all peoples to Myself." This verse has profound implications for understanding the inclusivity of Christ's mission. Early church father Origen argued that this drawing of all people indicates a future reconciliation, aligning with a hopeful perspective on salvation. Origen's interpretation suggests that Christ's crucifixion serves as a magnetic force, drawing all to the embrace of divine love.

We also have observed previously that Apostle Paul also speaks to the expansive nature of salvation in Romans 5:18-19 (KJV): "*Therefore, as through one man's offense judgment came to all men, resulting in condemnation, even so through one Man's righteous act the free gift came to all men, resulting in justification of life. For as by one man's disobedience many were made sinners, so also by one Man's obedience many will be made righteous.*" Paul's comparison here suggests a universal application of Christ's righteousness. Theologian N.T. Wright interprets this as evidence that the scope of salvation is as inclusive as the scope of sin, highlighting that just as sin impacted all, so too does Christ's redemptive act encompass all.

These passages collectively paint a picture of a God whose redemptive plans extend far beyond the limitations often imposed by human understanding, inviting us to grapple with the broader implications of His grace and mercy; which may imply possibility of hope of salvation for all.

The Impartiality of God

The New Testament emphasizes God's impartiality and the breadth of His grace, which extends beyond ethnic and religious boundaries. This theme is central to understanding the inclusivity of God's love and the nature of His salvation, which is offered to all humanity, transcending any divisions that humans may impose.

One pivotal passage that articulates this principle is found in Acts 10:34-35 (NKJV), which states, "Then Peter opened his mouth and said: 'In truth I perceive that God shows no partiality. But in every nation whoever fears Him and works righteousness is accepted by Him.'" This verse highlights the inclusive nature of God's acceptance and the absence of favoritism in His divine judgment. The early church father Irenaeus echoed this sentiment, asserting that God's salvation is intended for all people, irrespective of their ethnic or cultural backgrounds. He posited that God's desire is for all of humanity to come to know Him and experience His grace, explaining, "For it was in His goodness that He created all things, and thus He also saves those who come to Him from every nation."

Further illustrating the impartiality of God, Romans 2:6-11 (NIV) asserts: "who 'will repay each person according to what they have done.' To those who by persistence in doing good seek glory, honor, and immortality, He will give eternal life. But for those who are self-seeking and who reject the truth and follow evil, there will be wrath and anger. There will be trouble and distress for every human being who does evil: first for the Jew, then for the Gentile; but glory, honor, and peace for everyone who does good: first for the Jew, then for the Gentile. For God does not show favoritism." This passage emphasizes that God's judgment is fair and inclusive, applying to all individuals regardless of their background. The Apostle Paul highlights that God evaluates each person's actions and intentions rather than their lineage or status.

The consistent theme within this text reflects that God's judgment operates on the principles of justice and righteousness rather than human biases. Karl Barth elaborated on this concept in his monumental work, *Church Dogmatics*, where he argued that God's judgment is ultimately restorative rather than retributive. Barth emphasized that God's desire is to reconcile and restore humanity to Himself, as he stated, "The love of God is not only active in salvation but also in judgment, which is aimed at bringing about redemption." This view supports the notion that divine judgment serves a purpose that transcends mere punishment, aiming instead for the restoration of individuals to a right relationship with God.

Moreover, the impartiality of God is a recurring theme in the New Testament, reinforcing the understanding that salvation is accessible to all who seek Him sincerely. In Galatians 3:28, Paul asserts: "*There is neither Jew nor Gentile, neither slave nor free, nor is there male and female, for you are all one in Christ Jesus.*" This declaration embodies the essence of God's impartiality, emphasizing that in Christ, all distinctions that may divide humanity are rendered irrelevant in the context of salvation. It challenges any notions of exclusivity and reaffirms the idea that God's grace knows no bounds.

In conclusion, we can see that the New Testament presents a robust theological framework that underscores the impartiality of God. Through various scriptural references, we see a consistent message of inclusivity and the call to righteousness that transcends ethnic, cultural, and social barriers. The early church fathers and modern theologians alike have recognized and celebrated this divine attribute, urging believers to embrace a vision of salvation that reflects God's boundless grace and love. As we contemplate these truths, we are called to reflect the same impartiality in our interactions with others, embodying the love of Christ to all whom we encounter.

The Future Triumph of Christ

Scriptural promises suggest a future where Christ's victory will encompass a broad scope of humanity. This vision of universal reconciliation and triumph is a central theme in New Testament eschatology, where the ultimate sovereignty of Christ is affirmed, signaling a profound transformation of creation itself.

One of the foundational passages in this discussion is 1 Corinthians 15:24-28 (NKJV): "Then comes the end, when He delivers the kingdom to God the Father, when He puts an end to all rule and all authority and power. For He must reign till He has put all enemies under His feet. The last enemy that will be destroyed is death. For 'He has put all things under His feet.' But when He says 'all things are put under Him,' it is evident that He who put all things under Him is excepted. Now when all things are made subject to Him, then the Son Himself will also be subject to Him who put all things under Him, that God may be all in all." This passage encapsulates the eschatological hope of a future where Christ reigns supreme and every force opposing Him is vanquished. Thomas Torrance suggests that this passage envisions a scenario where the complete triumph of Christ includes the ultimate reconciliation of all things, asserting that "the very structure of the universe is designed to display the glory of God in the mediation of Christ." This perspective offers a hopeful outlook on the eventual restoration of creation, where all will be subject to Christ's authority, leading to a renewed reality where God reigns unchallenged.

In Philippians 2:10-11 (NKJV), we read: "That at the name of Jesus every knee should bow, of those in heaven, and of those on earth, and of those under the earth, and that every tongue should confess that Jesus Christ is Lord, to the glory of God the Father." This passage is powerful in its declaration that ultimately all beings, whether celestial, terrestrial, or infernal, will acknowledge Christ's lordship. Scholars such as F.F. Bruce interpret this as a universal acknowledgment of Christ, extending beyond the boundaries of this life and encompassing every creature. Bruce argues that this confession reflects not merely a future recognition of Christ's sovereignty but also aligns with the broader narrative of redemption woven throughout Scripture, suggesting that "the final victory of Christ is not just over sin and death but extends to every corner of existence."

Moreover, Revelation 7:9 (NKJV) provides a vivid depiction of the future triumph of Christ: "After these things I looked, and behold, a great multitude which no one could number, of all nations, tribes, peoples, and tongues, standing before the throne and before the Lamb, clothed with white robes, with palm branches in their hands." This verse paints a picture of inclusivity and the celebration of diverse peoples united in worship before God. Early church father Eusebius interpreted this vision as evidence of the ultimate inclusion of diverse peoples in God's final kingdom, stating, "The multitude represents the gathering of all who have been redeemed through Christ, transcending all boundaries that once separated humanity." This reinforces the notion that Christ's victory is not confined to a select few but rather embraces all of humanity, signifying that God's plan of salvation reaches every individual.

The theme of the universal scope of Christ's triumph is further echoed in the broader narrative of Scripture, where the redemptive work of Christ is presented as comprehensive and all-encompassing. It is this overarching vision of reconciliation that inspires hope among believers and challenges them to participate in the mission of the church: to share the good news of Christ's love and grace with all nations.

We can conclude that the New Testament provides a profound assurance of the future triumph of Christ that encompasses all of humanity. Through key scriptural passages, theologians and early church fathers affirm a hope that transcends current divisions, reflecting a God whose ultimate desire is the restoration of all creation. This eschatological promise not only informs our understanding of salvation but also compels believers to live in light of this hope, fostering a community that embodies the inclusivity of Christ's love.

The Hope for the Unevangelized and the Suffering

The question of hope for those who never had the opportunity to hear the Gospel or who suffered greatly is a deeply challenging and vital issue in contemporary theological discourse. This question can be approached through the lens of God's love and justice, emphasizing the belief that God desires the salvation of all humanity and is intimately concerned with the suffering of His creation. 1 Timothy 2:4 (NKJV) states, "who desires all men to be saved and to come to the knowledge of the truth." This verse reflects God's universal salvific will, suggesting an openness to redemption that transcends human boundaries and limitations. Theologian Jürgen Moltmann argues that this divine desire indicates a hopeful outlook for all humanity, noting that "the heart of God is inclined toward the salvation of all, and it challenges us to envision a reality where no one is beyond the reach of His grace." This perspective invites believers to consider that even those who have not heard the Gospel may still be embraced by God's love and grace, which operates in ways beyond human comprehension. In 2 Peter 3:9 (NKJV), we read: "The Lord is not slack concerning His promise, as some count slackness, but is longsuffering toward us, not willing that any should perish but that all should come to repentance." This verse emphasizes God's patience and His ultimate goal of universal repentance. Theologian Wolfhart Pannenberg highlights that God's longsuffering reflects His desire for all to come to knowledge and repentance, stating that "God's waiting is not a sign of indifference; rather, it embodies His active love and longing for reconciliation." This view reinforces the idea that even in suffering and isolation, God's intention remains focused on redemption, suggesting that He provides opportunities for repentance and transformation even in the most challenging circumstances. Moreover, Revelation 21:24 (NKJV) presents a vision of hope: "And the nations of those who are saved shall walk in its light, and the kings of the earth bring their glory and honor into it." This passage envisions a future where nations are not only saved but actively contribute to the glory of the New Jerusalem. The early church father Gregory of Nyssa interpreted this vision as evidence of the ultimate inclusivity of God's salvation, suggesting that "the glory of the nations signifies a broader scope of salvation that embraces diverse peoples in the eschatological fulfillment." This notion aligns with the understanding that God's ultimate plan encompasses not just individuals but entire nations, offering hope to those who may have lived and died without explicit knowledge of Christ.

In addition to these scriptural foundations, the discussions surrounding the hope for the unevangelized are enriched by considering the character of God as fundamentally loving and just. Many theologians posit that God's love cannot be confined to human understanding of evangelism and that His grace may operate in unseen ways. The potential for divine encounters and transformative experiences, even outside the traditional Gospel proclamation, remains a point of theological exploration.

The question of hope for the unevangelized and those who suffer is intricately tied to the character of God as loving and just. Through key biblical passages, theologians have articulated a vision of universal salvific intent that transcends human limitations and circumstances. The teachings of Scripture provide reassurance that God's desire for salvation is expansive and inclusive, inviting believers to embrace a hopeful outlook on the fate of those who may not have had the opportunity to hear the Gospel. This perspective not only inspires compassion for those who suffer but also encourages a faith that trusts in God's ability to bring about redemption in ways we cannot fully comprehend.

The Case for Hope Over Dogmatism

In the previous chapter and this chapter, we examined the challenging question of whether there is hope for those who find themselves in hell. This exploration highlighted the nature of God's love, mercy, and justice—central themes in the discourse on salvation and judgment. While infernalism presents a severe view of eternal punishment, and universalism offers a more optimistic outlook, it is crucial to recognize that an approach rooted in hope—rather than dogmatic assertions—aligns more closely with the broader narrative of Scripture. While universalism posits that all will eventually be saved, the evidence presented in Scripture suggests that a hopeful perspective—rather than a dogmatic universalism—may be more consistent with biblical teachings. The possibility of God's restorative justice should be considered, even if it is not dogmatically affirmed that all will be saved.

James 2:13 (NKJV) states, "For judgment is without mercy to the one who has shown no mercy. Mercy triumphs over judgment." This verse captures the essence of God's approach to judgment, emphasizing mercy over retribution. It reflects the divine inclination towards compassion and restoration, aligning with the notion that God's judgment is not solely punitive. Revelation 22:15-17 (NKJV) as we have discovered earlier further reinforces this theme: "For outside are dogs and sorcerers and sexually immoral and murderers and idolaters, and whoever loves and practices a lie. I, Jesus, have sent My angel to testify to you these things in the churches. I am the Root and the Offspring of David, the Bright and Morning Star. And the Spirit and the Bride say, 'Come!' And let him who hears say, 'Come!' And let him who thirsts come. Whoever desires, let him take the water of life freely." This passage suggests an open invitation to all, even those previously considered outside the bounds of grace. The imagery of an invitation to "come" reinforces a hopeful vision that transcends condemnation, welcoming even those that may have been judged into God's redemptive plan.

This perspective invites us to contemplate the fate of those who never had the opportunity to hear the Gospel or who have suffered greatly, echoing themes explored in previous chapters. It challenges us to consider that God's redemptive love may reach further than our limited understanding, affirming that His mercy might ultimately prevail. We can safely submit that, while infernalism and universalism offer contrasting views on the fate of those in hell, the scriptural evidence leans towards a hopeful perspective rather than a dogmatic stance. The expansive nature of Christ's redemption, the impartiality of God, and the eventual triumph of Christ suggest a broader application of salvation than traditionally conceived. The possibility of a restorative judgment, as opposed to a retributive one, aligns with a vision of God's love that transcends our immediate understanding. This hope encourages us to trust in the ultimate mercy and justice of God, reflecting the inclusivity of His redemptive plan. By fostering a spirit of compassion and hope, we can embody the love of Christ as we engage with the complex questions surrounding salvation and judgment.

Further Reading

1. Augustine of Hippo, *On the Trinity.*
2. Calvin, John. *Commentaries on the Gospel According to John.*
3. Origen, *De Principiis.*
4. Wright, N.T. *Paul and the Faithfulness of God.*
5. Irenaeus, *Against Heresies, Vol. 1.*
6. Barth, Karl. *Church Dogmatics, Vol. 2, Part 2.*
7. Torrance, Thomas. *The Mediation of Christ.*
8. Bruce, F.F. *The Epistle to the Philippians.*
9. Eusebius, *Ecclesiastical History, Book 3, Chapter 5.*
10. Moltmann, Jürgen. *The Trinity and the Kingdom.*

| 9 |

Living in the Light of Victory of Christ

As we conclude this exploration of eschatological themes, it is essential to draw connections between the profound theological insights we have examined and their implications for our daily lives. Understanding the nature of hell, the scope of salvation, and the ultimate victory of Christ is not merely an academic exercise but a call to live out the transformative power of the Good News. This chapter seeks to integrate these insights into a practical framework for living a victorious life in the present world.

The insights we have explored are deeply intertwined with our lived experiences. They compel us to consider how the truths of Scripture should influence our choices, interactions, and outlook on life. In a world filled with uncertainty, suffering, and moral ambiguity, the assurance of Christ's victory provides a firm foundation for navigating life's challenges. We are not just passive recipients of this Good News; we are called to actively engage with it, allowing it to shape our identities and guide our actions.

The Good News: A Comprehensive Vision

The Good News of Jesus Christ offers a holistic view of redemption that encompasses both the present and the future. The Gospel is not limited to a promise of eternal salvation but extends to a transformative impact on our lives here and now. It invites us to experience a radical change in our perspectives, relationships, and responsibilities, grounded in the reality of Christ's victory.

At the heart of the Gospel is the declaration that God is actively at work in the world, reconciling humanity to Himself through Jesus Christ. This reconciliation is not solely about individual salvation; it encompasses the restoration of all creation. Romans 8:21-22 reminds us that the creation itself will be liberated from its bondage to decay and brought into the freedom and glory of the children of God. This comprehensive vision of redemption shapes how we view our role in the world. We are called to be stewards of God's creation, actively participating in its healing and restoration.

Moreover, the Good News challenges us to rethink our understanding of success and fulfillment. In a culture that often equates worth with achievement and accumulation, the Gospel invites us to redefine success in terms of love, service, and faithfulness. This reorientation leads us to prioritize relationships over possessions, justice over convenience, and compassion over indifference. The transformative power of the Gospel urges us to engage deeply with the world around us, recognizing that our lives are testimonies to God's redemptive work.

The Triumph of Christ and Its Present Implications

The resurrection of Christ is the cornerstone of the Christian faith and signifies the ultimate victory over sin, death, and hell. This victory is not only a future promise but a present reality that empowers believers to live in the light of this truth. The resurrection assures us that death is not the end and that our lives are infused with purpose and hope.

1 Corinthians 15:54-57 (NKJV) encapsulates this truth beautifully: "So when this corruptible has put on incorruption, and this mortal has put on immortality, then shall be brought to pass the saying that

is written: 'Death is swallowed up in victory.' 'O Death, where is your sting? O Hades, where is your victory?' The sting of death is sin, and the strength of sin is the law. But thanks be to God, who gives us the victory through our Lord Jesus Christ." This passage celebrates Christ's victory and encourages believers to live in the confidence of this triumph.

The implications of Christ's victory permeate our daily lives, shaping our responses to fear, failure, and adversity. We are more than conquerors through Him who loved us (Romans 8:37). This declaration offers profound encouragement in the face of life's struggles. Rather than succumbing to despair or discouragement, we can draw strength from the knowledge that we are empowered by Christ's love to overcome challenges and obstacles.

Embracing a Life of Transformation

The Gospel invites us to experience transformation, moving from old patterns of behavior to a new way of living that reflects our identity in Christ. This transformation is both a personal and communal journey, marked by the fruit of the Spirit and a commitment to justice and love.

2 Corinthians 5:17 (NKJV) reminds us, "Therefore, if anyone is in Christ, he is a new creation; old things have passed away; behold, all things have become new." This transformation is not merely about behavioral change but a fundamental reorientation of our identity and purpose. As new creations, we are called to reflect the character of Christ in our thoughts, words, and actions.

Living out the fruit of the Spirit—love, joy, peace, forbearance, kindness, goodness, faithfulness, gentleness, and self-control (Galatians 5:22-23)—is evidence of this transformation. The presence of these qualities in our lives is a testament to the transformative power of the Gospel. When we embody these traits, we become beacons of hope and light in a world that desperately needs them.

Living Out the Victory in a Broken World

The present world is marked by suffering, injustice, and brokenness, but the Good News provides a framework for responding to these challenges with hope and action. As followers of Christ, we are called to be agents of change, bringing the light of the Gospel into the darkest corners of the world.

Matthew 5:14-16 (NKJV) reminds us of our calling: "You are the light of the world. A city that is set on a hill cannot be hidden." This call to be a light reflects our role in advancing the values of the Kingdom of God. Our actions and attitudes should draw others toward the hope and love found in Christ.

Moreover, James 1:27 (NIV) emphasizes the practical outworking of our faith: "Religion that God our Father accepts as pure and faultless is this: to look after orphans and widows in their distress and to keep oneself from being polluted by the world." This verse challenges us to engage in acts of compassion and justice, demonstrating our faith through tangible actions that reflect God's love for the marginalized and oppressed.

The Hope of Final Restoration

While the victory of Christ is a present reality, it also points to the ultimate hope of final restoration. The eschatological vision of a new heaven and new earth provides a future orientation that grounds our present experience in the assurance of God's ultimate plan.

Revelation 21:1-4 (NKJV) paints a vivid picture of this hope: "Now I saw a new heaven and a new earth, for the first heaven and the first earth had passed away... And God will wipe away every tear from their eyes; there shall be no more death, nor sorrow, nor crying." This vision of restoration assures us of God's ultimate redemption of creation and the promise of a future free from suffering and pain.

As we hold onto this hope, we are encouraged to persevere through our current trials, remembering that they are temporary in light of the eternal glory to come (Romans 8:18). This hope propels us to live with purpose and urgency, knowing that our efforts to embody the Good News contribute to God's overarching narrative of redemption.

Conclusion

The Good News of Jesus Christ, encompassing His victory over sin, death, and hell, is not just a future promise but a present reality that transforms our lives. As we have explored, this victory calls us to live in its light, embracing a life of transformation, hope, and active engagement in the world. By living out the implications of Christ's victory, we become agents of change, reflecting the values of the Kingdom of God in our personal lives and in our communities. The hope of final restoration anchors us in the assurance that God's redemptive plan will ultimately bring about a new creation where every tear will be wiped away.

As we move forward, let us embrace the Good News with renewed passion, allowing it to shape our identity, guide our actions, and inspire our mission. In doing so, we live out the victory of Christ in the present world, reflecting His light and love in all that we do. This holistic understanding of the Gospel not only enriches our faith but also compels us to share this transformative message with others, inviting them into the hope and victory that we have found in Christ.

ABOUT THE AUTHOR

Samuel Sanni is the President of Supernatural Life Forum, a ministry dedicated to reaching the world with the transformative message of hope and inclusion based on the finished work of Christ. Through various media platforms, including YouTube teachings, social media, outreach, books, blogs, and music, Samuel shares the profound love of God and the message of Christ's all-encompassing grace.

Sam is a gifted teacher of the unadulterated Gospel of Christ, unafraid to delve into topics often avoided in mainstream Christendom. His teachings emphasize the centrality of Christ, His victorious work on the cross, and the boundless love of God, inviting everyone to experience the freedom and life found in Him.

He is joyfully married to Ola, and they are blessed with two wonderful children, Agape and Charis. When he's not writing, Sam enjoys listening to and creating music and spending quality time with his family and friends. He is also an avid reader, continually exploring the works of both classic and contemporary authors.